SIGNAL

SIGNAL

Understanding What Matters in a World of Noise

STEPHEN FEW

Analytics Press

BURLINGAME, CALIFORNIA

Analytics Press

PO Box 1545
Burlingame, CA 94011
SAN 253-5602
www.analyticspress.com
Email: info@analyticspress.com

PUBLISHER: Jonathan G. Koomey

COPY EDITOR: Nan Wishner
COMPOSITION: Bryan Pierce
COVER DESIGN: Keith Stevenson
PRINTER AND BINDER: C&C Offset Printing Company

ISBN: 978-1-938377-05-1

This book was printed on acid-free paper in China.

10 9 8 7 6 5 4 3 2

To those who work tirelessly, with little notice, to make sense of data and deliver its message clearly and truthfully. You are my heroes. It is in your honor and for your benefit that I've written this book.

ACKNOWLEDGEMENTS

The ideas expressed in this book have been drawn from the works of many, especially (in alphabetical order) Stacey Barr, William Cleveland, Frederick Hartwig, Nate Silver, John Tukey, Charles Wheelan, and Donald Wheeler. I would also like to thank my friend Alberto Cairo for constantly asking how the book was coming along and for recommending many fine books to consult along the way.

CONTENTS

PREFACE

I began working in information technology (IT) over 30 years ago. After less than one year of working part time for a chain of Computerland stores, I joined a large semiconductor manufacturer in Silicon Valley as its one and only personal computer (PC) consultant. I worked in a small group called Decision Support (DS), which belonged to a division called Corporate Information Systems (CIS) before the term "IT" came into routine use. I had not prepared for this job in college. Instead, I'd earned a bachelor's degree in Communication Studies and a Master's degree in Religious Studies and then had gone on to begin doctoral studies in the history and phenomenology of religion (a fancy name for comparative religions). As a student in the social sciences with my heart set on a lifetime of work as a professor, I never imagined that I could work for a corporation, and I had no desire to do so. However, after seven and a half straight years of university studies while working part time waiting tables in a restaurant and then later as a sales clerk in a bookstore, I was burned out and tired of being poor. So I became one of the original corporate PC nerds. I had no idea at the time where that decision would eventually take me.

What qualified me to work in a group that helped people use information to make business decisions? I knew nothing about semiconductor manufacturing, only slightly more about business, and not a thing about turning data into knowledge to support decisions other than what I'd picked up as a student. What was this corporation thinking when it hired me?

The answer to this question requires some historical context. At the time, the PC was brand new and still unfamiliar. It had only begun making its way into the business world a year or so earlier. I was hired as a PC consultant because I knew a little more than how to flip on the power switch of this new-fangled device, and that was more than most other people knew. I used an original IBM PC (the one with a single floppy disk drive) to type my master's thesis and then spent nine months developing and teaching PC software courses, but that was the sum total of my experience. Real PC experts were not available for hire at the time.

This episode in the early days of my career illustrates a problem that has plagued organizations since the advent of the PC and in many respects has worsened over time. People are sometimes hired for a particular job merely because they know how to use software that was designed to support the kind of work done in that job. It is assumed that if a person knows how to use software designed to do something in particular, that person must also already possess the skills that the software was designed to support. This, however, is not the case. This naïve expectation is an expression of *technological solutionism*, an epidemic that has infected our age. Technology does not solve problems; people do. Can you imagine yourself willingly going for a heart transplant under the knife of a surgeon who was trained in using surgical tools but knew nothing about the body, including your heart?

IT tools can at best assist us in performing work that we already understand. Computers can augment, but not replace, the skills of knowledge workers and decision makers. Despite what some technologists and many science fiction plots lead us to believe, computers can't think and might never acquire this ability.

The *information age* continues to exceed our grasp. At best, we live in the *data age*. We have made great strides in accumulating data. By comparison, we have made little progress in using data to inform better decisions.

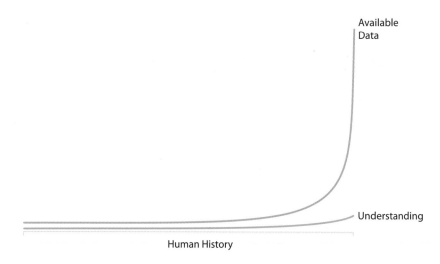

FIGURE 1

Even though it feels as if we're progressing at light speed today, we're not actually making much headway. This is because we're investing our attention and energy in the wrong things. We keep chasing the latest information technologies, foolishly believing IT vendors and thought leaders when they authoritatively proclaim that we can't survive without the latest tools. There's a word for these proclamations: *marketing*. It's in the interest of vendors and thought leaders to keep us believing that we'll be left behind unless we invest in the newest technologies, but it is often not in our interest to do so. As long as we continue to focus our attention on each new IT development as if it is a panacea, feverishly loading more data in storage as fast as possible, we'll remain ignorant and exhausted, naively mistaking a flurry of inconsequential activity for progress. Data can only inform better decisions if we find and understand the significant messages that reside in it. Data sensemaking involves skills that don't come automatically; they must be learned. Without these skills, information technologies are useless. I've written this book to help us learn these skills.

Hundreds of books have already been written about statistics, but few have been written about the kinds of data analysis that should be *routinely done* in organizations. Most data analysis courses provide instruction in specific software products, not in the skills that are required to use those products effectively.

Based on recent headlines, we might think that many organizations are making great progress in becoming analytically adept, but this isn't the case. According to Randy Bartlett:

Some might object to my use of the term "data" as a singular rather than a plural noun. Although in Latin the word *data* is the plural form of *datum*, when "data" originally entered the English lexicon in the 17th century, it was commonly used in both the singular and plural form. To correct someone for using data as a singular noun is unjustified, no more appropriate than correcting them for using "agenda" rather than "agendum." For more on this, see the essay by Daniel Rosenberg, "Data before the Fact," in *"Raw Data" Is An Oxymoron* (2013). Edited by Lisa Gitelman. MIT Press.

Corporations are not as sophisticated or as successful as we might grasp from the sound bytes appearing in conferences, books, and journals. Instead opinion-based decision making, statistical malfeasance, and counterfeit analysis are pandemic. We are swimming in make-believe analytics.

Randy Bartlett (2013). *A Practitioner's Guide to Business Analytics*. McGraw-Hill, page 10.

I've worked with many of the organizations that have grand reputations for analytical prowess and have found that, despite small pockets of expertise here and there, in general these organizations remain analytically naïve. They're still struggling with the basics. Unfortunately, there aren't many people to whom they can turn for practical help.

Donald Wheeler describes the imbalance between the needs and skills that currently exist in the workplace from the perspective of a veteran who has seen it all.

Businessmen are finding that while they have more numbers than ever before, they still do not know what these numbers mean. If the numbers changed for the better compared to last month, then just wait—they will change for the worse soon enough. If the numbers actually changed for the worse compared to last month, then the apocalypse is at hand and all is doomed! The boss is in despair—"Don't just stand there, do something!" You have to come up with an explanation of why the numbers were so bad, or else find a scapegoat, by 10:30 tomorrow morning. Moreover—how are you going to keep these bad numbers from happening again? How are you going to get the workers to work harder? "And Pharaoh said, 'You are lazy! You will be given no straw, but you must produce the same tally of bricks each day.'" And so it goes, month after month, world without end. From the dawn of time until the present, there is nothing new under the sun— just more of it...This deficiency has been called "numerical naiveté." Numerical naiveté is not a failure with arithmetic, but it is instead a failure to know how to use the basic tools of arithmetic to understand data. Numerical naiveté is not addressed by the traditional courses in the primary or secondary schools, nor is it addressed by advanced courses in mathematics. This is why even highly educated individuals can be numerically naive.

Fortunately, the cure for numerical naiveté is very simple. The principles are easy to grasp and the techniques are very easy to implement.

Donald J. Wheeler (2000). *Understanding Variation*, Second Edition. SPC Press, pages v-vii.

Understanding cannot be found in technologies or in the frantic accumulation of more data. It can only be found by observing things that matter and using our brains to understand and respond to these things. The means of detecting and measuring signals in data are well within reach when we rely on the right resources, however rare those might be. This book is my attempt to make these means readily available and easy to understand.

After writing three books in the field of data visualization, which together provide an introduction to the use of visualization for data exploration, analysis, and presentation, I asked "What next?" To answer this question, I tried to determine what was still needed that I could possibly provide. What would the people who had read all three of my books most need to further enrich their use of data? With this question never far from my thoughts, over time I began to notice that even those with a good grasp of the fundamentals that I taught often spent time wandering in the data forest, not quite sure what they should be seeking. They knew how to look at data and how to present it to others, but they didn't always know what deserved their attention most. Stated differently, they didn't know how to separate the signals from the noise. Eventually, this became the focus of my work and the content of this book. Only the signals matter.

Steve

INTRODUCTION

Data contains descriptions. Some are true, some are not. Some are useful, most are not. Skillful use of data requires that we learn to pick out the pieces that are true and useful. All creatures, not only humans, perceive and process data to make their way in the world. Data existed long before we humans entered the scene. On the African savannah when our species was young, we survived because we developed the means to separate signals from noise in data better than our competitors. It was this ability that allowed us to rise to the top of the heap, but we won't remain on top if this ability declines and we become overwhelmed by noise.

Human perceptual and cognitive abilities have evolved in uniquely powerful ways. We can think abstractly, pass on what we learn through language, and make tools—technologies—to extend our reach. These abilities have enabled us to develop extraordinary signal detection skills, but they've also enabled us to generate a great deal of noise. Presently, the noise is increasing much faster than our ability to filter it.

Although we have always been extraordinary data processors, today we claim to value data more than ever and have built a powerful and influential industry to promote its use. Digital information technologies are still in their infancy. We have much to learn, and as we learn, we're making mistakes. Foremost among these mistakes, we are investing too much confidence in the information technologies that we've created. We tend to think of "Technology" with a capital "T," the panacea of our age, rather than a collection of small "t" technologies—some good, many poor, and sometimes used properly but often not. We've forgotten that technologies are the products of our own making and that they possess no power that we haven't built into them. It is we, not our machines, who think. Using modern information technologies effectively requires perceptual and cognitive skills that must be learned. When we forget this, we stumble and waste our technological potential. Sometimes, we even do harm.

Apart from the secondary benefits of digital data, which are many, such as faster and cheaper information collection and distribution, the primary benefit is better decision making based on evidence. Despite our intellectual prowess, when we allow our minds to become disconnected from reliable information about the world, we tend to screw up and make bad decisions.

Big Data, Little Information

Organizations throughout the world are accumulating huge and rapidly growing stores of digital data, but their ability to use data to improve decision making has progressed little and in some respects has regressed. When we rely on information technologies to think for us, our ability to think for ourselves atrophies, at times resulting in downright stupidity. Take a moment to remember the last time you spoke to a telephone support person who couldn't think beyond the scripted responses that appeared on his screen. "Are you not listening to me?" you might have screamed! Machines are stupid, and people who rely on machines to do their thinking for them behave stupidly as well. What a shame. Nate Silver understood this when he wrote:

> *We face danger whenever information growth outpaces our understanding of how to process it. The last forty years of human history imply that it can still take a long time to translate information into useful knowledge, and that if we are not careful, we may take a step back in the meantime.*

Nate Silver (2012). *The Signal and the Noise*. Penguin Press, page 7.

> *If the quantity of information is increasing by 2.5 quintillion bytes per day, the amount of useful information certainly isn't. Most of it is just noise, and the noise is increasing faster than the signal. There are so many hypotheses to test, so many data sets to mine—but a relatively constant amount of objective truth.*

Ibid., page 13.

The world is getting noisier as we embrace the visions of the digital titans who reap wealth and power from unrelenting data growth. Ralph Waldo Emerson was insightful when he wrote, "There are many things of which a wise man might wish to remain ignorant." There is no value in noise.

Ralph Waldo Emerson (1883). *Lectures and Biographical Sketches.*

The term *data*, unlike the related terms *facts* and *evidence*, does not connote truth. Data is descriptive, but data can be erroneous. We tend to distinguish data from *information*. Data is in a primitive or atomic state (as in "raw data"). It becomes information only when it is presented in context, in a way that informs. This progression from data to information is not the only direction in which the relationship flows, however; information can also be broken down into pieces, stripped of context, and stored as data. This is the case with most of the data that's stored in computer systems. Data that's collected and stored directly by machines, such as sensors, becomes information only when it's reconnected to its context.

In and of itself, data has no value. At best, it has potential. Celebrating data for its own sake is silly. Data becomes valuable when it informs us of something useful that matters. Until then, it is noise. Not long ago I gave a keynote presentation at a large conference in Dublin, Ireland. At one point while wandering through the Dublin Convention Center, I noticed a banner with the following words spoken by Fred Smith, the chief executive officer (CEO) of FedEx:

> *There's more to shipping than shifting containers. The information about the package is as important as the package itself.*

This was one of many banners strategically placed throughout the convention center to promote the conference. When I read Smith's words, I suddenly had an epiphany about why my packages occasionally arrive damaged or late. Apparently the shipping company believes that the data it collects, generates, stores, and tracks about my package is as important as the package itself.

Seriously? In our enthusiasm for data and the technologies that support its use, some of us have lost perspective. Data about a package in transit is valuable if it helps the shipping company get that package to its destination on time and intact. It has no value in and of itself.

This book is about detecting and making sense of the meaningful and useful information—the signals—that reside in the midst of noisy data. Detecting and making sense of these signals is challenging because most data is noise. Signals in data are the exception, not the rule. This is especially true today.

Signal detection has been getting harder with the advent of so-called Big Data. By its very nature, most data will never amount to anything but noise. Collecting everything possible—based on the Big Data argument that the costs of doing so are negligible and that even data you can't imagine being useful today could become useful tomorrow—is a dangerous strategy. The costs of collecting and maintaining everything extend beyond the hardware that's used to store data. People are already struggling to use data effectively and having a harder time as the volume of data grows. As we turn up the volume of noise, it becomes increasingly difficult to hear anything meaningful. It's like a radio that's stuck on static between channels at maximum volume. If only we could turn the dial to find a clear channel. Finding a needle in a haystack doesn't get easier as we're tossing more and more hay on the pile.

The Nature of Signals

A signal is a useful message that resides in data. Data that isn't useful is noise. The graph below suggests that there is a relationship between ice cream sales and violent crimes, but this relationship is spurious. Both ice cream sales and violent crimes increase during seasons of hot temperatures. The message of this graph is noise because it misinforms.

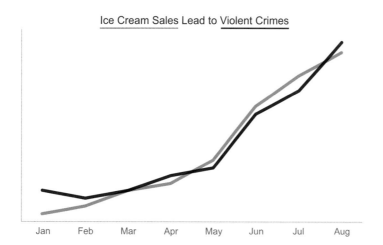

Ice Cream Sales Lead to Violent Crimes

FIGURE 2

When data is expressed visually, noise can exist not only as data that doesn't inform but also as meaningless non-data elements of the display (e.g., irrelevant attributes, such as a third dimension of depth in bars, color variation that has no significance, and artificial light and shadow effects). In the graph below, the data might be useful, but there's no way to tell because the visual noise of the three-dimensional planes and colors in the display obscures any message that the data might contain.

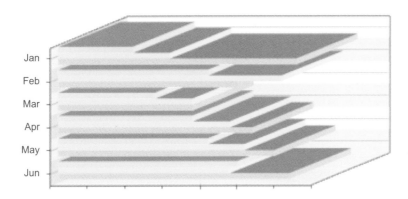

FIGURE 3

We must filter out these sources of noise to find and process actual signals in the data.

Donald Wheeler, an accomplished data sensemaker, says "The difference between signals and noise is the foundation for every meaningful analysis of data." He goes on to say:

Donald J. Wheeler (2000). *Understanding Variation*, Second Edition. SPC Press, page 30.

> *Unfortunately, most managers are proud of their ability to interpret noise as if it were signal. They consider this to be an art.*

Ibid., page 111.

When we rely on data for making decisions, how do we tell what qualifies as a signal and what is merely noise? In and of itself, data is neither. Assuming that data is accurate, it is merely a collection of facts. When a fact is true and useful, only then is it a signal. When it's not, it's noise. It's that simple.

For a fact to be useful, it must:

- Inform
- Matter
- Deserve a response

When any of these qualities are missing, data remains noise. Did we learn something we didn't already know from the data? Do we understand what we learned? If so, we have been informed. Does what we learned have value, and can it make a difference? If so, it matters. Should we do something about it? If so, we've encountered a signal.

Signals always point to something. In this sense, a signal is not a thing but a relationship. Data becomes useful knowledge of something that matters when it builds a bridge between a question and an answer. This connection is the signal.

Signals can be divided into two basic types:

1. Exploratory signals
2. Signals of change

When we approach a new data set, we begin by getting the lay of the land, exploring and looking for signals that help us understand the context. An understanding of what's routine gives us context for detecting what's unusual.

Everything that informs us of something useful that we didn't already know is a potential signal. If it matters and deserves a response, its potential is actualized. We're confronted with many signals in the beginning because we're starting from almost total ignorance about the data set. However, once we've developed a basic understanding of a data set—an overview of routine versus unusual behavior—signals from that point on become rare, and most new signals reveal themselves as changes. These signals surface in the following three forms:

- Significant changes in patterns
- Significant changes in magnitude
- The appearance of a known and significant pattern

When a pattern shifts from the norm, that's potentially a signal. When the range within which values routinely vary changes in shape, contracts, or expands, that's potentially a signal. When a specific pattern that we recognize as a harbinger of good or ill fortune appears, that's potentially a signal. In this book, we'll learn to prime our senses for signals of all three types.

Signals will always represent a problem that we might be able to fix or an opportunity to achieve something desirable. Opportunities come in two flavors:

- Direct opportunities, such as a great sales lead
- Indirect opportunities, such as extraordinarily good outcomes that are being achieved by others (e.g., unusually few incidents of post-surgical infections at a particular hospital) that we can learn to apply for ourselves

Most people who are responsible for data sensemaking have never been trained to detect signals. An insidious assumption exists, promoted by software vendors, that knowing how to use their tools "auto-magically" imbues users with the skills of a data analyst. Even with good software—a rare commodity—this is not true. As in any area of expertise, data analysis requires training and practice, practice, practice...and more practice. Because relatively few people possess the necessary skills in most organizations, much time is wasted and money lost as we pore over data without knowing what to look for. We fritter away time pursuing patterns that are meaningless and missing those that are priceless.

The signal detection techniques that we'll rely on in this book focus on change through time, especially on methods that have been developed for *statistical process control*. In *Chapter 9 – Install Signal Sensors*, we'll learn these methods at a basic level and then apply them to data of all types.

The Slow Data Movement

To focus effectively on signal detection, I propose that we shun Big Data and embrace the "Slow Data Movement." In 1986, Carlo Petrini founded the "Slow Food Movement," which began as resistance to the opening of a McDonald's fast-food restaurant near the Spanish Steps in Rome. I've seen this affront to the old city myself and felt the disgust that must have emboldened Petrini to start what soon became an international movement. Slow Food was introduced as an alternative to fast food. It embraces the belief that much of the benefit of food requires that we take time with it: time in producing it, time in preparing it, and time in savoring it as we eat. The Slow Food Movement is now part of a broader "Slow" movement that focuses on many aspects of life. For instance, there is a Slow Reading Movement that encourages people to slow down and appreciate what they read. It is not surprising that, in our fast-paced world, slowing down and embracing life with greater awareness and appreciation would become something we need to cultivate, lest we forget who we are and what makes life worth living. I believe that we should extend the Slow Movement to the realm of information technology. In this time of so-called Big Data, too much is being missed in our rush to expand our data stores. The entire point of collecting data—using information to better understand our world and make more informed decisions—has been forgotten and is certainly not being achieved in the manic rush to throw more technology at a problem that can only be solved by slowing down and thinking more deeply.

Big Data is usually defined in terms of the 3Vs: volume, velocity, and variety. Doug Laney of Gartner originally defined the 3Vs 13 years ago. Even at that time the 3Vs were already old news. I remember reading Laney's paper shortly after publication and thinking that he did a good job of characterizing significant aspects of data that had been true since the advent of the computer. Actually, if we want to be historically accurate, we can date the beginning of Big Data to the year 1440 when Gutenberg invented the printing press. The advent of the printing press had a greater impact on the world of information in terms of volume, velocity, and variety than the advent of computers. For that matter, long before the printing press, the invention of writing had an even greater impact and before that the invention of language even greater. In other words, what's happening with data today has roots firmly planted in a long line of developments that have allowed humans to disseminate information through the ages. Technologies increase data volume, velocity, and variety. The fact that data has increased in these ways at an exponential rate since the advent of the computer is well known and has been for years, yet, packaged as Big Data by software vendors, this ongoing growth is suddenly being embraced as something new and unprecedented. Hurray data! Hurray technology! Three cheers for the technology vendors that are making a bundle selling incremental extensions of what they've been selling all along. While the world reaches for its wallet amidst the rising clamor, what's important about data is being lost in the din.

For those who mostly rely on open-source rather than commercial software, as is often the case in non-profit, government, or academic organizations, the Big Data bombardment of marketing hype might not have a direct effect. If you are in this category, consider yourself lucky, assuming that the software tools you use are reliable. Those of you in this camp might also be thinking that you are missing a significant change that has been ushered in by Big Data: the ability to forego data sampling because it is now possible to work with huge, complete data sets. If you've relied on sampling in the past because of technological impediments, then you have legitimate reason to celebrate the elimination of this limitation. What you might not realize, however, is that the use of huge, entire data sets has been common practice in some organizations for many years. I've been helping large corporations, such as banks, insurance companies, and telecommunications companies, use vast data sets in full for my entire career. These organizations never considered sampling data that was readily available in full. Sampling still makes sense when data collection involves a time-consuming and costly effort, but when entire populations of data are readily available or easily accessible, technology imposes few limitations today. The deceit of Big Data is the claim that this is new (although it may be new for you) and that it has radically changed the ways in which we make sense of data.

I'd like to introduce a set of goals that should serve as counterpoints to the 3Vs as we struggle to welcome the elusive information age. May I present the 3Ss: small, slow, and sure.

As data increases in volume, we should keep in mind that only a relatively small amount of data is useful. Data consists of much noise and relatively little signal. We must separate the signals from the noise, which we'll never get around to doing if we spend all of our time boosting technology for data generation and collection rather than learning how to find and understand what's actually meaningful and useful.

According to many advocates of Big Data, increases in data volume eliminate the need for data quality. One measure of data quality is its signal-to-noise ratio: the higher the ratio of signal to noise, the better the quality. However, many advocates of Big Data, especially vendors who sell Big Data products, argue that more data is inherently better. It's in their interest to make you think this is true. The authors of *Big Data: A Revolution That Will Transform How We Live, Work, and Think* espoused this position when they wrote:

> *In a world of small data, reducing errors and ensuring high quality of data was a natural and essential impulse. Since we only collected a little information, we made sure that the figures we bothered to record were as accurate as possible…Analyzing only a limited number of data points means errors may get amplified, potentially reducing the accuracy of the overall results…However, in many new situations that are cropping up today, allowing for imprecision—for messiness—may be a positive feature, not a shortcoming. It is a tradeoff. In return for relaxing the standards of allowable errors, one can get ahold of much more data. It isn't just that "more trumps some," but that, in fact, sometimes "more trumps better."*

Viktor Mayer-Schönberger and Kenneth Cukier (2013). *Big Data: A Revolution That Will Transform How We Live, Work, and Think.* Houghton Mifflin Harcourt, pages 32–33.

"More trumps better" is an ignorant claim. It's hard to imagine circumstances when "more" offers advantages over "better." In the realm of food, people choose more over better only when they've never tasted better. Until you've had good food, you only care about filling your stomach. As long as you have an adequate supply of good food, would you ever prefer a bigger helping of bad food? "Bigger is better" is a common American theme, but it is hardly a virtue. I've never met skilled data analysts who select data based on volume. Instead, they select the data that they need (i.e., the right data) and is reliable (i.e., good quality data), in the amount that serves their purpose (i.e., enough data, sometimes in the form of a random sample).

We're in love with speed. Like many people, I love to drive fast. It's a rush. Much of what I value in life, however, requires time. I must slow down. This is especially true of data sensemaking and decision-making. Lao Tzu, the founder of Taoism, said: "Muddy water, let stand, becomes clear." These words have come to mind—and to the rescue—many times in my life. I recently read a new book titled *Wait: The Art and Science of Delay* by Frank Partnoy, which roots the benefits of waiting, pausing, and taking a bit more time, in science. In the introduction Partnoy says:

> *Given the fast pace of modern life, most of us tend to react too quickly. We don't, or can't, take enough time to think about the increasingly complex timing challenges we face. Technology surrounds us, speeding us up. We feel its crush every day, both at work and at home. Yet the best time managers are comfortable pausing for as long as necessary before they act, even in the face of the most pressing decisions. Some seem to slow down time. For good decision-makers, time is more flexible than a metronome or atomic clock...As we will see over and over, in most situations we should take more time than we do.*

Frank Partnoy (2012). *Wait: The Art and Science of Delay.* Public Affairs, pages xi–xii.

Although some decisions in life are best made instantly, based on intuition, this is only true if our intuitions come out of a great deal of relevant experience and the matter at hand does not lend itself to time-consuming deliberation, such as a bear running toward us at full speed. These are the types of decisions that Malcolm Gladwell wrote about in *Blink*. Most non-routine decisions, especially those that change the courses of our lives, benefit from conscious, deliberate, analytical reasoning—what Daniel Kahneman calls "System 2 Thinking." Kahneman refers to our two modes of reasoning as thinking fast (System 1) and thinking slow (System 2):

> *The division of labor between System 1 and System 2 is highly efficient: it minimizes effort and optimizes performance. The arrangement works well most of the time because System 1 is generally very good at what it does: its models of familiar situations are accurate, its short-term predictions are usually accurate as well, and its initial reactions to challenges are swift and generally appropriate. System 1 has biases, however, systematic errors that it is prone to make in specified circumstances...It sometimes answers easier questions than the one it was asked, and it has little understanding of logic and statistics.*

Daniel Kahneman (2011). *Thinking, Fast and Slow.* Farrar, Straus and Giroux, page 25.

> *The defining feature of System 2...is that its operations are effortful... System 2 is the only one that can follow rules, compare objects on several attributes, and make deliberate choices between options. The automatic System 1 does not have these capabilities. System 1 detects simple relations ("they are all alike," "the son is much taller than the father") and excels at integrating information about one thing, but it does not deal with multiple distinct topics at once, nor is it adept at using purely statistical information.*

Ibid., page 36.

One of the great data sensemakers of the last 100 years was a statistician named John Tukey who taught at Princeton University. Tukey was known for taking his time. When he was engaged as a consultant to solve a problem, he would begin by listening carefully and asking questions to clarify the issues.

Next, he would remain silent for a long time, often alone in his hotel room for a day or two. Eventually, he would emerge to provide an answer. His answers were thoughtful.

No matter how quickly data is generated and transmitted, the act of data sensemaking, which must precede its use, is usually a slow process. We must take time to understand information and act upon it wisely. Speed will, in most cases, lead to mistakes.

Even though we can collect data about everything imaginable, variety is not always a boon. More choices are helpful only if we need them and have the time and means to consider them. Otherwise, they do nothing but burden our already overly complicated lives. More than variety, we need data that is sure-footed, as in reliable and useful. In an effort to remain sane and productive, I spend a fair amount of time limiting my choices. For instance, I don't participate in *Twitter*, instant messages, *Facebook*, or even the professional social networking service *LinkedIn* because I already handle enough interactions with people as it is. By restricting myself mostly to email and direct face-to-face conversations, I maintain a level of human interaction that works for me. I'm not suggesting that these services are bad; they just don't suit me. The next time you're in a grocery store browsing the toothpaste section, ask yourself if all those choices arranged in daunting rows are useful. Wouldn't just a few sure choices make life simpler?

Our lives are rich in variety. This can be a good thing. Data provides collections of facts about life and the world, but only a subset of those facts will be ever be useful. The same is true for our organizations. Just because we can collect data about something doesn't mean we should. In fact, given all the data that we've already collected, wouldn't it make sense to spend more time making use of it rather than being wrapped up in the acquisition of more? When we recognize an opportunity to do something useful with data, that's when it becomes sure. As people and organizations of limited resources, shouldn't we spend our time identifying what's useful and then actually using it?

Data is growing in *volume*, as it always has, but only a *small* amount of it will ever function as signals. Data is being generated and transmitted at a faster *velocity*, but this isn't a race; *slow* thinking is required for sensemaking. Data is branching out in ever-greater *variety*, but only a few of these new choices are *sure*. Small, slow, and sure must be our focus if we really want to use data more effectively to create a better world. I doubt that my 3Ss will ever become the rallying cry of a popular movement, but those who heed them will become the true heroes of the information age. When the dust settles, we'll see that people who took their time to be thoughtful with a limited set of the right data were the ones who solved the problems of our age.

The Goal of Data Sensemaking

The immediate goal of data sensemaking is understanding. When a statistician analyzes the results of a medical experiment to determine whether a hypothesis is true, she is usually trying to understand a correlation among variables, perhaps one that is causal in nature. But why does she care? Because that understanding might lead to better medical treatments that could save lives.

Understanding isn't the ultimate goal; better decision-making and action is. We analyze data not just so that we can better understand the world, but so that we can use our understanding to make the world better.

Despite all the talk today about advanced analytics and evidence-based decision-making, we're still not very good at it. The kinds of thinking and skill that are required don't come naturally. According to Derrick Niederman and David Boyum, this is definitely true in America.

> *Most Americans are poor quantitative thinkers. This widespread innumeracy is the father of zillions of bad decisions, and you don't need DNA testing to confirm its paternity. Numbers convey information, quantitative information. Decisions are based on information. When people are innumerate—when they do not know how to make good use of available quantitative information—they make uninformed decisions.*

Derrick Niederman and David Boyum (2003). *What the Numbers Say: A Field Guide to Mastering Our Numerical World.* New York: Broadway Books, page 229.

A solution to this deficiency won't be easily achieved, and it certainly won't come in the form of a new technology. Most of the skills and techniques that are required to use data more effectively for decision-making have been around for years. Almost everything that I present in this book has been known since I first started working in information technology 30 years ago. The latest technologies are often sexy, but beware of solutions that vendors dress up like trollops, unless you're looking for a one-night stand.

We must get this right. It's time to slow down, learn the basics, and invest our time and resources in proven methods. Kahneman points out that most organizations do a deplorable job of preparing for their most essential work.

> *Whatever else it produces, an organization is a factory that manufactures judgments and decisions. Every factory must have ways to ensure the quality of its products in the initial design, in fabrication, and in final inspections. The corresponding stages in the production of decisions are the framing of the problem that is to be solved, the collection of relevant information leading to a decision, and reflection and review.*

Daniel Kahneman (2011). *Thinking, Fast and Slow.* Farrar, Straus and Giroux, page 418.

Not very sexy? We need to get over it. The sooner we accept this, the sooner we'll start making better decisions.

Few organizations make decisions that have more potential for enormous success or horrendous disaster than government intelligence organizations. How can they improve the intelligence that they pass on to decision makers? Here's what Richard J. Heuer, Jr., a leading CIA analyst who wrote the manual for analyst training, has to say:

> *How can intelligence analysis be improved? That is the challenge. A variety of traditional approaches are used in pursuing this goal: collecting more and better information for analysts to work with, changing the management of the analytical process, increasing the number of analysts, providing language and area studies to improve analysts' substantive expertise, revising employee selection and retention criteria, improving report-writing skills, fine-tuning the relationship between intelligence analyst and intelligence consumers, and modifying the types of analytical products.*

Richard J. Heuer, Jr. (2006). *Psychology of Intelligence Analysis.* Novinka Books, page 180.

Any of these measures may play an important role, but analysis is, above all, a mental process. Traditionally, analysts at all levels devote little attention to improving how they think. To penetrate the heart and soul of the problem of improving analysis, it is necessary to better understand, influence, and guide the mental processes of analysts themselves...More training time should be devoted to the thinking and reasoning processes involved in making intelligence judgments, and to the tools of the trade that are available to alleviate or compensate for the known cognitive problems encountered in analysis.

Ibid., page 184.

Heuer's advice applies equally well to organizations of all types that rely on data analysis for decision making. The solution lies within us, specifically in our heads.

Learning to See

What I do, in a nutshell, is teach people to think more effectively about data and to clearly, simply, and accurately communicate what they learn. Most of the skills that I teach involve *data visualization*. This isn't because I'm predominantly a visual thinker. In fact, my natural thinking style is verbal; I love words. So why do I study, practice, and teach data visualization? Because some types of thinking and communication are best done visually. Some information cannot be expressed with words in a way that leads to understanding, yet a simple picture does the job beautifully. Graphical displays of quantitative data—numbers—in the form of graphs make it possible for us to see and understand facts, patterns, concepts, and relationships that aren't otherwise accessible. Graphs also make it possible for us to compare entire series of values. For example, a line graph with one line for a year's worth of monthly domestic sales revenues and another for international sales revenues would make it possible to compare them at a glance and immediately see how they differ, both in magnitudes and patterns of change through time. The same 24 numbers displayed in a table would sit silent, not revealing this information, despite great effort even by someone who considers himself a "numbers guy." Many of the best methods for detecting and understanding signals in data involve using our eyes.

Colin Ware, the world's leading expert in visual perception as it applies to data visualization, says:

Why should we be interested in visualization? Because the human visual system is a pattern seeker of enormous power and subtlety. The eye and the visual cortex of the brain form a massively parallel processor that provides the highest-bandwidth channel into human cognitive centers. At higher levels of processing, perception and cognition are closely interrelated, which is the reason why the words 'understanding' and 'seeing' are synonymous. However, the visual system has its own rules. We can easily see patterns presented in certain ways, but if they are presented in other ways, they become invisible...The more general point is that when data is presented in certain ways, the patterns can be readily perceived. If we can understand how perception works, our knowledge can be translated into rules for displaying information. Following perception-based rules, we can present our data in such a way that the important and informative patterns stand out. If we disobey the rules, our data will be incomprehensible or misleading.

Colin Ware (2012). *Information Visualization: Perception for Design,* Third Edition. Morgan Kaufmann Publishers, page xxi.

Vision is by far our most powerful sense. Fifty percent of the brain's resources are dedicated to vision. Seventy percent of the sense receptors in the human body reside in the retinas of our eyes. Perceptually, we are predominately visual creatures, yet most of us fail to tap the majority of our visual thinking potential. Some people are exceptional visual thinkers. Temple Grandin, who has done amazing work to improve the treatment of cattle, is autistic, but her brain compensates through its extraordinary ability to hold and manipulate images. It has been said of the scientist Nikola Tesla that he could envision and run tests on entire systems in his head, working out the bugs before beginning to build the real thing. By comparison to these extraordinary visual thinkers, most of us, myself included, make only rudimentary use of the great potential for visual thinking that is embedded in the structure of our brains. However, we can compensate for what we cannot hold and manipulate in our heads by using technologies that help us construct and manipulate visual images on a screen. This is how data visualization technologies augment our ability to think. Edward Tufte, one of the most respected leaders in data visualization, once wrote: "Clear and precise seeing becomes as one with clear and precise thinking." Data visualization provides a unique and powerful means to scale new heights in understanding.

Edward R. Tufte (1997). *Visual Explanations.* Graphics Press, page 53.

Another exceptional data sensemaker, statistician William Cleveland, places visualization at the center of data analysis.

Visualization is critical to data analysis. It provides a front line of attack, revealing intricate structure in data that cannot be absorbed in any other way. We discover unimagined effects, and we challenge imagined ones.

William S. Cleveland (1993). *Visualizing Data.* Hobart Press, page 1.

Cleveland, and John Tukey before him, were both leading statisticians who challenged the status quo by promoting the essential role of graphics in statistics. Frustrated with unnecessary limitations that the statistical community had long imposed, Tukey and Cleveland led efforts to break free from these bonds by emphasizing "data analysis" as their term of choice to distinguish what they promoted from traditional statistics. Statistical calculations and graphical displays collaborate to support quantitative analysis. Each has its own strengths and limitations. In this book, I will tightly weave the best of statistics and data visualization into a collaborative toolkit for detecting and interpreting signals.

Stewardship

A *steward* is someone who is responsible for overseeing and protecting something that's believed to be worthy of care and preservation. Some stewards look after a household, some a tract of land. Others take on responsibilities that are broader in scope, such as caring for the environment at large. A steward is an apt metaphor for a good data sensemaker. We strive to detect and understand signals in data for a purpose: to protect, preserve, and improve the well-being of the people, organization, or other concerns that we serve. When we care about something, we take time to become familiar with it. The better we understand something, the better able we become to care for it.

The metaphor of stewardship frames the content of this book. Let's think of ourselves as stewards into whose hands the care for a land and its people has been placed. This is a privilege that we choose to embrace with utmost vigilance. The land and its people are revealed to us through a collection of data. In the beginning, the land is unfamiliar. We must get to know it before we can determine the conditions that require our care and the signals that will keep us informed of those conditions. Once those signals are known, we must watch tirelessly for them. Whenever we detect them, we must respond with decisions and actions that serve the interests of the land. In the real world in which we work as data sensemakers, the land and its people might serve as a metaphor for a portfolio of products that our company manufactures and the customers to whom they're sold, or perhaps as the staff and facilities of a hospital along with the sick patients who enter the hospital from which they hope to depart healthy. Whatever the purpose of the organization or cause that we serve, we will serve it well if we approach the work as good stewards, faithful and true.

In the world of data sensemaking, it would be rare for one person to be responsible for the full range of tasks, from surveying the data landscape in the beginning to making the ultimate decisions that are needed. Nevertheless, even if we never personally make decisions in response to signals in data, we must fully understand the process from beginning to end and approach our work as caretakers. We will learn to search for signals as if the land depends on us and us alone for its well-being. We will learn to become trusted stewards, equipped both with good intentions and the skills needed to fulfill them.

To find signals in data, we must learn to reduce the noise—not just the noise that resides in the data, but also the noise that resides in us. It is nearly impossible for noisy minds to perceive anything but noise in data. Most of the work that we must do to become good data stewards is done within. Only when we can still the inner storm of random thoughts can we see past the randomness that resides in data. Although practices and approaches for stilling our internal thought processes are beyond the scope of this book, they are worthwhile to pursue. As we begin discussing, in the next chapter, how to orient ourselves in a new land of data, I think we'll see how thinking deliberately—slowly and surely—aids us in detecting the signals from which we will develop an overview of the land that will, in turn, form the context for detecting the signals we'll use to monitor the well-being of the land.

PART I GET TO KNOW THE LAND

We've just arrived in the land for the first time after a long flight. Exhausted, but curious and excited, we stand outside the airport terminal amid the bustle of an unfamiliar culture. The air is alive with possibilities as we breathe it in deeply, exhale, and smile. We'll only begin this particular journey once, and we're determined to do it well. The data beckons. What now? What first?

We've been entrusted with the care of the land. In the next eight chapters, we'll learn how to become familiar with it. Quality care requires deep knowledge. We'll find that the land will reveal itself when we explore it in particular ways, each designed to bring different aspects of its nature into focus.

Part I of this book, "Get to Know the Land," is over twice the length of Part II, "Watch Over the Land." Although we'll encounter exploratory signals while becoming familiar with the land, most of what we'll do during this process will build the understanding that will serve as context for detecting signals of change, which is the focus of Part II. Confucius said, "Success depends upon previous preparation, and without preparation there is sure to be failure." Part I is dedicated to the work that we must do to prepare for signal detection. More recently, in the 19th century, Abraham Lincoln said, "Give me six hours to chop down a tree and I will spend the first four sharpening the axe." This is unpopular but sage advice. Here in Part I, we will sharpen our axes.

1   SURVEY THE LAND

As eager stewards, we're dying to lay our eyes on the data, but we must wait a little longer. Before diving in, some preparation is in order. If we were traveling to a country we'd never visited before, we might prepare by consulting guidebooks, travel articles, and friends who had been there, to get background information and tips on how things work in that foreign place. Here we begin in a comparable way, getting to know the organization whose data we'll be analyzing.

What, How, and Why

Before exploring an organization's (or cause's, product's, etc.) data, we must first get to know the organization's essential reason for being (*what* it does, *how* it does it, and *why*):

- *What* entities (e.g., products or services) characterize the organization's mission?
- What processes reveal *how* the organization does what it does?
- What values explain *why* the organization does what it does?

We must understand the entities (what), processes (how), and values (why) of the organization before we can begin to understand the data that reveals the organization's performance and well-being.

Just as uninformed travelers can misunderstand foreign cultures, we could be the most talented data analysts in the world, but if we know little about the domain that we're analyzing, we'll waste time and misunderstand much that we observe. We can't evaluate how an organization is doing without first understanding what matters to the organization. This knowledge equips us to distinguish what's meaningful and important (signals) from the mounds of data that matter little or not at all (noise). Signals only materialize within the context of a specific purpose, specific objectives, and a sense of what matters. To equip ourselves to distinguish signals from noise, we must begin our journey here.

We won't accomplish this in a day. It takes time to become familiar with the work of an organization more deeply than simply examining the veneer of its professed mission and objectives. We needn't worry that we might never know the organization as well as those who have worked there for years. Coming from the outside with fresh eyes offers some advantages. When people become entrenched in their work, they tend to lose perspective. When they work in the trenches, it becomes difficult to see the landscape that surrounds them and they might lose sight of the bigger picture. They often do what they do because that's how they've always done it. When this happens, they tend to find in data what they expect to find. They can use our fresh eyes to help them find what's actually there.

If possible, we should start with an organization's leaders. We want to understand the perspective of the people in charge. This perspective will give us a useful framework on which to hang the details that we'll learn from others. To understand a process, we must also spend time with those who actually do the work because what actually happens is often quite different from what those in charge believe. We will ask questions and observe. If we can, we'll seek opportunities to do some of the work ourselves. In addition to deepening our understanding in useful ways, this will also give those whom we're trying to help a reason to trust us.

Entire books have been written about this process, so we won't cover it in detail here. For the purposes of this book, our focus is on studying a map of the territory that the people who live and work there will draw for us. The map is not the territory—we'll no doubt find errors—but it will give us a sense of direction and orientation as we venture into the data on our own, and it will give us a structure for the information we collect during our process of discovery.

With this preparation done, we can begin our journey.

Data Vistas

A few years ago I traveled to Adelaide, Australia for the first time. To my great delight, I was met at the airport by Bryan King of the Government of South Australia, who had organized the workshop that I would teach there. I travel a great deal, and it isn't often that I'm met at the airport and driven to my hotel by one of my hosts, especially a high-ranking public servant. Before heading to the hotel, Bryan drove me to the top of a hill that is the highest vantage point in Adelaide. As we enjoyed the vista, Bryan pointed out the city's major sites, helping me get a sense of the place.

FIGURE 1.1 Photo of Adelaide, Australia, by Doug Barber.

Because of this experience, even though I've only been to Adelaide twice, I know that city much better than many others that I've visited more often. The lesson of this story is that when we want to get a sense of an unfamiliar place, we should initially head for high ground.

Analytical journeys are quite different from leisure travel. Tourism involves a series of destinations where we hope to enjoy ourselves. We want to add sweet memories to our lives—great meals, beautiful sights, and interesting people that we meet along the way. When we embark on an analytical journey, however, we don't pre-plan all of our destinations, and we're not just collecting memories. The goal of the analytical journey is a thorough understanding of the territory, with the goal of ultimately solving problems and seizing opportunities. We approach the analytical journey as if we're preparing to become tour guides, able to explain each site in a way that extends from its history to predictions about its future. We must learn to navigate like a native.

Too often data analysts make the mistake of getting lost in the details without first taking time to get the lay of the land. Without an overview—the big picture—we lose our orientation in the midst of data. An overview gives us context and makes it possible for us to maintain an awareness of how the details fit into the larger whole.

Several years ago, Ben Shneiderman, a respected pioneer in the fields of information visualization and human-computer interaction, proposed a simple formula for exploring and analyzing data: "Overview first, zoom and filter, then details-on-demand." We who work in the field of information visualization refer to these words affectionately as *Shneiderman's Mantra*. Although Shneiderman's brief expression doesn't describe all aspects of data sensemaking, he has it right that we should always begin with an overview of unexplored territory before venturing into the forest.

Ben Shneiderman (1996). "The Eyes Have It: A Task by Data Type Taxonomy for Information Visualizations." *Proceedings of the 1996 IEEE Symposium on Visual Languages.*

Actually, we will be doing something more than exploring. Effective data analysis combines the skills of an *explorer* and a *detective*: a little bit of Lewis and Clark mixed in with a bit of Sherlock Holmes. Exploration comes first; before beginning the work of an attentive sleuth, we explore to get our bearings. To do this, we don't just wander aimlessly. The purpose of our exploration is to construct a summarized overview of the territory—a mental model—in our heads. To understand a collection of data, our brains must structure it.

To structure data, we distill from it a representative set of characteristics that describe it overall. We can only hold a few pieces of data in our heads before we need a framework on which to begin hanging them. Descriptive statistics were developed for this purpose. Charles Wheelan writes:

I'm amused when software vendors talk about *unstructured data analysis*. This doesn't make sense. To make sense of unstructured data, we must first structure it.

> *From baseball to income, the most basic task when working with data is to summarize a great deal of information…The irony is that more data can often present less clarity. So we simplify. We perform calculations that reduce a complex array of data into a handful of numbers that describe those data, just as we might encapsulate a complex, multifaceted Olympic gymnastics performance with one number: 9.8.*

> *The good news is that these descriptive statistics give us a manageable and meaningful summary of the underlying phenomenon...The bad news is that any simplification invites abuse.*

Charles Wheelan (2013). *Naked Statistics*. Norton, page 17.

Wheelan warns that the simplified overview that we obtain from descriptive statistics is insufficient in and of itself. We need more. William Cleveland expands on this point:

> *Many techniques of data analysis have data reduction as their first step. For example, classical statistical procedures, widely used in science and technology, fall in this category. The first step is to take all of the data and reduce them to a few statistics... Then, inferences are based on this very limited collection of values. Using only numerical reduction methods in data analyses is far too limiting. We cannot expect a small number of numerical values to consistently convey the wealth of information that exists in data.*

William S. Cleveland (1994). *The Elements of Graphing Data*. Hobart Press, page 8.

As Cleveland makes clear, a set of descriptive statistics alone is not enough. It will always fail to reveal critical facts. But we need to reduce a data set to something that is both accurate and manageable for our first exploration of the territory that it encompasses. So what do we do?

This brings us to the purpose of this book, which is to help us understand how we can use data visualization techniques to detect and work with meaningful signals in a data set. Critical facts that lie hidden in data can only be seen in a picture. This is true not only for our task in this chapter, surveying the data when we first begin to study it, but for the subsequent detective work we will do as we analyze the data, and ultimately for our work as stewards monitoring the signals we find in the data for the purpose of monitoring the organization's well-being.

Our ability to obtain an accurate overview of any data set depends on the quality and accuracy of the data visualization techniques we use for this purpose. Let's look at an example.

Imagine that we want to understand the composition of our customer base according to their ages. We already know that the average age of our customers is 33 years. Is this enough? All three of the histograms on the following page summarize a distribution of people by age with an average age of 33 years.

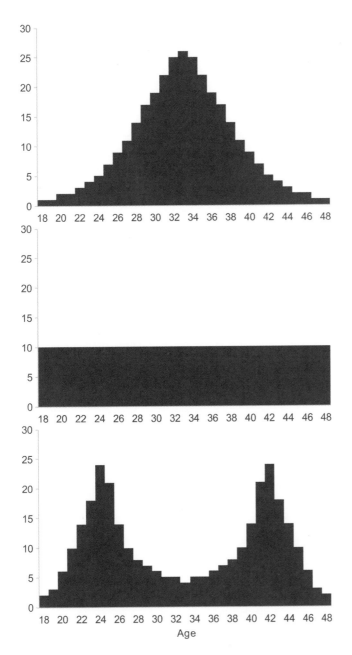

FIGURE 1.2

We can easily see from these three graphs that the average alone is not enough for us to understand the composition of our customer base, but would the addition of more statistics provide the information that's revealed in the graphs above? For example, if we knew the standard deviation of our customers' ages (i.e., the degree to which they vary around the mean of 33 years), would that give us what we need? It would give us more, but not enough. We wouldn't know the shape of the distribution, which is essential because the shape tells an important story.

The importance of a distribution's shape is clearly illustrated by the *Anscombe Quartet*, which consists of four sets of eleven paired values from two variables, displayed in the following scatter plots to reveal the relationship between the variables:

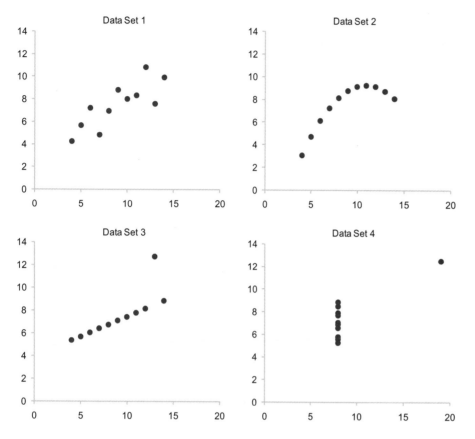

FIGURE 1.3. F. J. Anscombe (Feb 1973). "Graphs in Statistical Analysis." *American Statistician*, Volume 27, pages 17-21.

As we can see, the shapes of these relationships differ considerably, but when they're described using statistical summaries alone, such as means and correlation coefficients, they don't differ at all. So we ask the question again: what do we do to ensure that our data visualization methods open up meaningful vistas for exploring the data landscape? Each of the next six chapters will focus on data visualization and interaction techniques for building an overview that gives us a reliable roadmap for all further analysis and signal detection.

Context, Context, Context

An overview does more than give us a summary; it also gives us context for understanding the details of a data set. Signals can only be detected in context—that is, in comparison to other relevant information. Edward Tufte once said, "At the heart of quantitative reasoning is a single question: *Compared to what?*" Too many errors occur because decisions are made after looking at data without sufficient context. Noticing that this week's sale revenues are lower than last week's and then berating the sales staff on this basis alone is foolish. Last week's sales alone don't provide enough context to assess the team's performance.

Edward R. Tufte (1990). *Envisioning Information*. Graphics Press, page 67.

Donald Wheeler regards the importance of context as the first principle of data sensemaking.

No data have meaning apart from their context.

Three consequences of this first principle are:

- *Trust no one who cannot, or will not, provide the context for their figures.*
- *Stop reporting comparisons between pairs of values except as part of a broader comparison.*
- *Start using graphs to present current values in context.*

Donald J. Wheeler (2000). *Understanding Variation*, Second Edition. SPC Press, page 13.

When we survey a land, we begin to understand its norms: how it usually looks and behaves. This sense of normality—what's routine—can then serve as a backdrop against which signals—often departures from the norm—will stand out.

Context, context, context. I can't over-emphasize the importance of context. Without it we're flying blind.

Data Fitness

The general pattern formed by the distribution of a variable's values, or by the relationship between two variables' values, is called the *fit* or *fit model*. For example, a trend line that summarizes the essential shape of data in a scatter plot—the nature of the co-relationship (i.e., correlation) between two quantitative variables—is called a *line of best fit* or sometimes a *curve of best fit*.

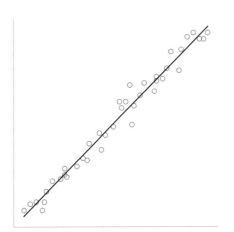 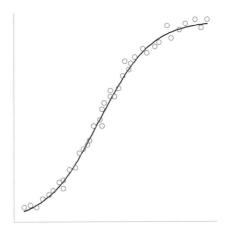

FIGURE 1.4

A fit model summarizes the overall nature, the dominant pattern, of a distribution or correlation. It doesn't describe data in detail; it doesn't show every value in the set. The degree to which a particular fit model accurately describes a data distribution or correlation is called its *goodness of fit*.

Another name for fit is *smooth*. This is because a fit model smooths out the rough edges or jaggedness in the data to capture the essence of the data set. Statistical algorithms that determine a fit model are sometimes referred to as *smoothers*. Just like Goldilocks when she visited the home of the three bears, we're looking for a fit that feels just right—not too soft and not too hard. If the fit is too soft (too smooth), important aspects of the data's essential nature will be missed. If the fit is too hard (not smooth enough), so much detail will be shown that the overall nature of the data will be difficult to discern.

Differences between the fit model and the actual values are called *residuals*. When we add up all of the differences between each value and the fit model, if the sum of the residuals is small, the values align closely with the fit, which means that the fit does a good job of describing the overall nature of the data. In a scatter plot, residuals are measured as the vertical distance of each data point from the fit line or curve.

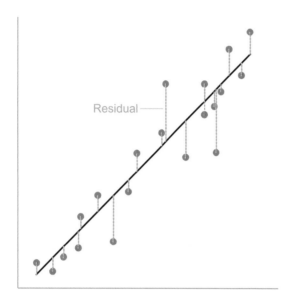

FIGURE 1.5

Fit is a high-level summary of the shape of a data set, and residuals are the extent (i.e., from a little to a lot of variation) to which the values differ from that summary and the manner (i.e., the shape of variation) in which the values differ from the summary. This gives us the following formula:

$$data = fit + residuals$$

Most residuals fall within the range of routine variation; those that fall outside this range are called *outliers*. We explore data to determine the fit and residuals as well as the boundaries beyond which residuals are no longer routine and qualify as outliers. Once these boundaries of routine variation (fit plus nearby residuals) are established, they provide context for further data analysis, making it easy to spot outliers, which are often signals.

Variation and Relationships

Individual items of data are units of description. These descriptions are either categorical (items in a category, such as products or countries) or quantitative (measures of something, expressed as numeric values, such as sales revenues or blood pressure). To understand data, we must examine both the categories and the measures that are associated with them. The diagram below shows a few examples of categories and measures that would typically be important to a sales organization:

Categories	Customer	Order	Time	Territory	Product	Warehouse

Measures	Profit	Units Sold	Customer Satisfaction	Shipment Past Due	Revenue	Expense

FIGURE 1.6

Meanings are found in variations within categories and measures and in relationships among these elements. Variation and relationships usually fall into one of the following six types:

1. **Variation within categories**

   How do items in important categories (customers, hospitals, etc.) relate to one another in magnitude (i.e., based on tallies and measures associated with them), especially their rank order (*ranking relationships*, e.g., lowest to highest) and the degree to which each contributes to the whole of the category (*part-to-whole relationships*)?

2. **Variation within measures**

   How are values within important measures distributed across the range from lowest to highest (*distribution relationships*)?

Two categories in particular—space and time—are especially revealing and warrant individual attention.

3. **Variation across space**

   Where are values located in space relative to one another (*spatial relationships*)?

4. **Variation through time**

   How do values change through time (*time-series relationships*)?

Many interesting stories reside in the meaningful and sometimes predictable ways in which measures relate to one another.

5. **Relationships among measures**

   How do measures behave in relation to one another (*correlations*)?

Other interesting stories reside in the ways in which categories relate to one another.

6. **Relationships among categories**

   How do categories relate to one another, mediated by measures (*intercategory relationships*)?

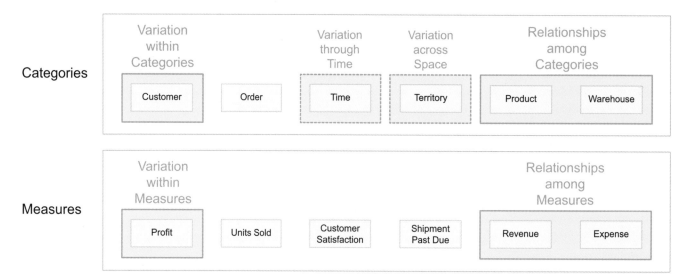

	Variation within Categories		Variation through Time	Variation across Space	Relationships among Categories	
Categories	Customer	Order	Time	Territory	Product	Warehouse

	Variation within Measures				Relationships among Measures	
Measures	Profit	Units Sold	Customer Satisfaction	Shipment Past Due	Revenue	Expense

FIGURE 1.7

These six fundamental types of variation and relationships are the focus of the next six chapters where we'll go over each in detail.

By examining these specific types of variation and relationships, we can build an overview of the data that will function as a background against which we'll be able to coax signals into the foreground. Fortunately, our senses are highly evolved for detecting subtle differences and patterns, but we must learn what to look for, to hone our ability to detect meaningful differences and patterns among the noise.

One ubiquitous example of noise is *randomness*. Without training in statistics, we tend to mistakenly ascribe meaning and significance to random variation. We waste time when we fret over random variation because we can neither predict nor control it since it has no identifiable cause. Derrick Niederman and David Boyum describe the situation this way:

> *A crucial first step is to develop a healthy respect for the power of randomness. The notion that many events have no assignable cause is surprisingly difficult to accept. Perhaps that's because randomness gets confused with disorder and meaninglessness, both of which are discomforting to most of us. Our brains would rather create nonexistent patterns than be without patterns altogether. But the fact remains that much of what happens in the world is the product of chance. If we don't learn to appreciate the enormous influence of chance, we will regularly read too much into events and in so doing leap to conclusions that aren't justified.*

Derrick Niederman and David Boyum (2003). *What the Numbers Say: A Field Guide to Mastering Our Numerical World*. New York: Broadway Books, page 198.

As we focus in the next six chapters on the types of variation and relationships listed above, we'll develop a standard toolkit of graphs and data interactions for each one. The tools in this toolkit will help us reveal and clarify the essential nature of the data and enable us to distinguish noise from variation that matters.

The Science of Data Analysis

I mentioned earlier that a data analyst combines the skills of an explorer and a detective. Scientists also combine these skills to learn about the world. The scientific method was developed to produce a reliable understanding of the world. During the Enlightenment, the development of the scientific method led to an exponential growth in knowledge and technology that we are still experiencing today. As data analysts, we must adapt and apply the scientific method to our work. Richard J. Heuer, Jr. explains why this is important:

> *Scientific method is based on the principle of rejecting hypotheses, while tentatively accepting only those hypotheses that cannot be refuted. Intuitive analysis, by comparison, generally concentrates on confirming a hypothesis and commonly accords more weight to evidence supporting a hypothesis than to evidence that weakens it. Ideally, the reverse would be true. While analysts usually cannot apply the statistical procedures of scientific methodology to test their hypotheses, they can and should adopt the conceptual strategy of seeking to refute rather than confirm hypotheses.*

Richard J. Heuer, Jr. (2006). *Psychology of Intelligence Analysis.* Novinka Books, pages 60–61.

Far too often, we begin with an assumption (hypothesis) and seek only to confirm it. This biased approach produces findings that match our expectations instead of uncovering what's actually there.

> *Analysis of competing hypotheses involves seeking evidence to refute hypotheses. The most probable hypothesis is usually the one with the least evidence against it, not the one with the most evidence for it. Conventional analysis generally entails looking for evidence to confirm a favored hypothesis.*

Ibid., pages 116–117.

The scientific approach to data analysis is used in the diagnostic work of medical doctors.

> *The doctor observes indicators (symptoms) of what is happening, uses his or her specialized knowledge of how the body works to develop hypotheses that might explain these observations, conducts tests to collect additional information and evaluate the hypotheses, then makes a diagnosis. This medical analogy focuses attention on the ability to identify and evaluate all plausible hypotheses. Collection is focused narrowly on information that will help to discriminate the relative probability of alternate hypotheses.*

Ibid., pages 74–75.

Carefully designed scientific experiments typically test a single hypothesis. Regulated industries, such as pharmaceutical companies, are often required to run at least two large-scale studies with a single primary hypothesis before obtaining approval to market a drug for a specific illness. While we likely can't apply this level of rigor in many business analyses, we should keep in mind that conclusions drawn from analyses that test many hypotheses simultaneously may be misleading because of a lack of adequate controls.

   Instead of using the Big Data approach—collecting everything possible, hoping to find some pattern or way to make the pieces fit together to tell a story—we must approach data intelligently, allowing our knowledge of the domain to guide us to information that is relevant and meaningful. We must consider everything that might explain the conditions that we observe; we can't accept the first explanation that comes to mind. We must step back and reconsider again and again as we examine data, looking for potential explanations that we haven't already considered. Like medical doctors and scientists, we search for the truth, including truths that are unexpected or unwelcome.

The Explorer's Journal

When Lewis and Clark explored the new territory that was acquired by the United States from France through the Louisiana Purchase, they kept separate journals of their travels. While reading the rich records of their journey, I was able to imagine myself in that vast, uncharted wilderness west of the Mississippi River. As data explorers preparing for our work as stewards, we'll emulate their example. We won't need to produce a beautiful work of literature for the ages, but we must document our findings as an aid to memory and a gift to posterity.

Keep in mind that we're constructing an overview of the territory that will serve as context for all subsequent analyses, especially for detecting signals. This written record will help us build a clear summary of the data that will supplement and reinforce the conceptual models that we carry in our heads. Later, in *Chapter 11 – Document the Land*, we'll consider a way to record our findings.

2 VARIATION WITHIN CATEGORIES

I usually begin analytical journeys by examining variation within important categories. Categories provide the conceptual framework on which we can hang almost all of the information that we gather during the rest of our journey. Although signals reside in measures, not categories, signals almost always relate to categories. For example, an uncharacteristic drop in sales revenue (a measure) may be tied to one or more specific categorical items, such as particular geographical regions. Sales revenue overall might concern us, but behavior at a lower level in association with one or more categories is probably driving the higher-level problem. On the flip side, overall sales revenue might look just fine, but something might be terribly amiss deeper down at the categorical level.

Let's get familiar with variation within important categories. Because we already gathered a general working knowledge of the organization's domain by our interactions with experts and other survey activities in the previous chapter, we can narrow the list of categories to those that are most intimately related to the organization's work and goals. For a typical sales organization, this list might consist of the following categories:

- Customer
- Region
- Time
- Product (or Service)
- Sales Channel
- Sales Representative

For a typical hospital, the following categories might appear on the list:

- Patient
- Department
- Time
- Diagnosis
- Procedure
- Physician
- Outcome

Each category has important stories to tell about its parts: how they relate to one another and the whole. Two relationships in particular will interest us most as we examine variation within categories: ranking and part-to-whole relationships.

Ranking and Part-to-Whole Relationships

The first relationship that interests us when we look at a list of items belonging to a category, such as a list of products, is how they differ (from most to least or vice versa) in association with an important measure. Categorical items in and of themselves don't express quantitative values. In fact, they mean relatively little until they're tied to a quantitative measure. By itself, a list of product names isn't very interesting. As soon as we associate it with a measure, such as sales revenue, however, it comes alive.

Product	Revenue ($)
Amaretto	26,269
Caffe Latte	35,899
Caffe Mocha	84,904
Chamomile	75,578
Colombian	128,311
Darjeeling	73,151
Decaf Espresso	78,162
Decaf Irish Cream	62,248
Earl Grey	66,772
Green Tea	32,850
Lemon	95,926
Mint	35,710
Regular Espresso	24,031

FIGURE 2.1

The products that sell most impress us with their performance. Those that sell least concern us. These relationships are easy to see when the list is arranged in ranked order.

Product	Revenue ($)
Colombian	128,311
Lemon	95,926
Caffe Mocha	84,904
Decaf Espresso	78,162
Chamomile	75,578
Darjeeling	73,151
Earl Grey	66,772
Decaf Irish Cream	62,248
Caffe Latte	35,899
Mint	35,710
Green Tea	32,850
Amaretto	26,269
Regular Espresso	24,031

FIGURE 2.2

When we view this ranked list of products graphically, as in the bar graph on the following page, other characteristics come to light, such as the significant difference between the first- and second-highest-selling products.

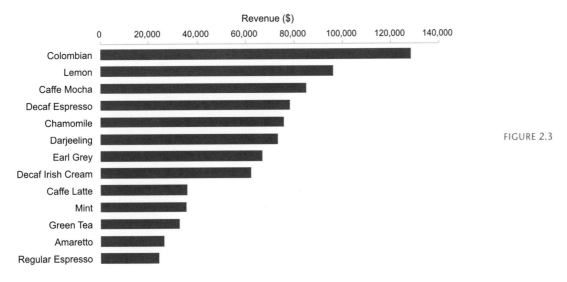

FIGURE 2.3

A ranked list takes on new meaning when we consider how each item contributes to the whole. In the graph below, revenues are now expressed as percentages of total sales, which makes it easy to understand each product's contribution.

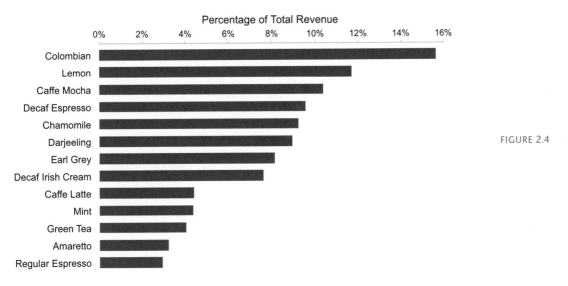

FIGURE 2.4

The fact that sales of the top two products contribute about 27% of total revenues is now a part of the product story that we can add to our developing overview.

To explore ranking and part-to-whole relationships within categories, we're going to use a particular set of graphs that will feature tallies (how many?), sums (how much?), and means (how much per item on average?).

Charts of Tallies, Sums, and Averages

We'll deal with the special and uniquely important categories of space and time separately in later chapters. For now, let's continue to use product as an example. "Product" is a category usually associated with higher-level categories in a hierarchical arrangement. For example, products might belong to product types, which in turn belong to product lines. Assuming this particular hierarchy, it would make sense to begin exploring product information at the highest level: product line. Imagine that our organization sells coffees and teas that are organized into two product lines: beans and leaves. Already knowing that the tally (count) of product lines is two, let's move down one level in the hierarchy to find out how many product types belong to each product line. We can begin by examining this simple set of tallies in a table.

Product Line	Product Type Tally
Coffees	2
Teas	2

FIGURE 2.5

Each product line consists of two product types. We can tally the next level in the hierarchy—individual products—as well.

Product Line	Product Type	Product Tally
Coffees	Coffee	3
	Espresso	4
Teas	Herbal Tea	3
	Tea	3

FIGURE 2.6

When we explore a category that's structured hierarchically, it's natural to tally the items in a lower-level category that are associated with a higher-level category. Tallies aren't limited to rigid hierarchies, however. Tallies apply whenever it's useful to count the number of items in any category that's associated with another category. For example, if we were analyzing the performance of hospitals (category 1), we might count the distinct medical procedures (category 2) that were performed on individual patients (category 3). We could also do the opposite: for each patient (category 3), we might count the number of procedures undergone (category 2) per hospital (category 3). Tallying items in one category that are associated with items in another category is a common task when we're exploring data.

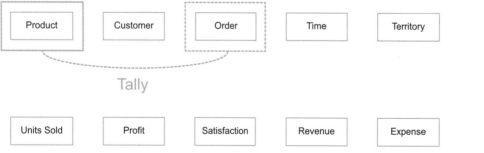

FIGURE 2.7

Earlier, we used a table to view the tally of product types within product lines, which worked fine because the list of items was small. In many cases, however, the lists are much longer, so the easiest and quickest way to compare values is to view them in either a bar graph or a dot plot. We'll start with a bar graph that tallies products within product types and product lines, from greatest to least.

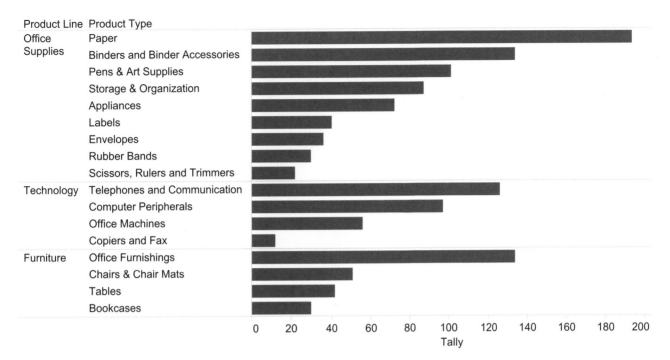

FIGURE 2.8

The same data appears below as a dot plot.

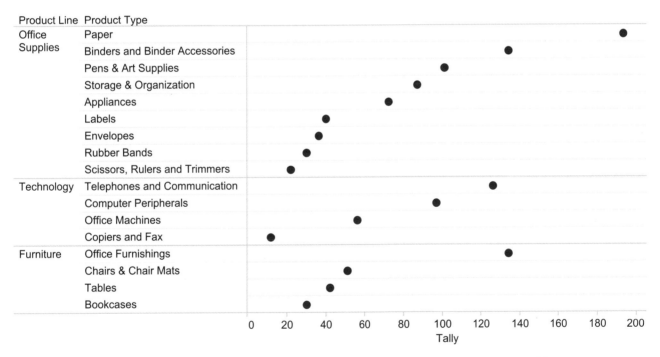

FIGURE 2.9

Both graphs make it easy to see each value precisely, to compare individual values, and to get a quick sense of the entire data set. Dot plots are particularly useful when all of the values fall within a relatively narrow range far from zero. In bar graphs, zero must serve as the baseline for bars because their lengths (horizontal bars) or heights (vertical bars) represent the values but can only do so accurately when the bars begin at zero. If the bars start from any value other than zero, their relative lengths or heights do not accurately represent the relative values. Unlike bar graphs, the quantitative scales in dot plots do not need to begin at zero, which allows us to zoom in exclusively on the quantitative range that contains the values without having to provide the space that would be needed to extend the scale down to zero. This is illustrated in the example below.

FIGURE 2.10

In the dot plot of tallies in Figure 2.9 on the previous page, we can easily see that our organization sells several more office supply products than technology and furniture products. This doesn't necessarily mean that most of its revenues are associated with office supplies, however. To answer the question of where revenues come from, we can switch from a tally to sum.

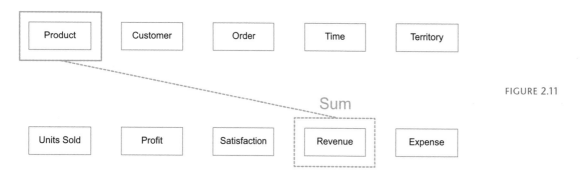

FIGURE 2.11

Here's the sum of revenues per product type:

FIGURE 2.12

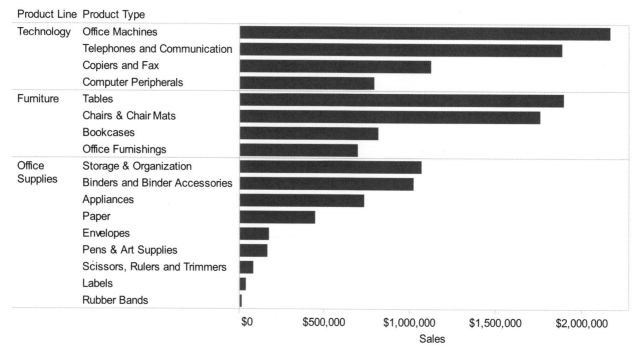

Even though the company offers twice as many office supply products as either technology or furniture products, we can now see that more revenues per product are earned from technology sales. To examine this more easily, we can switch from sums to averages.

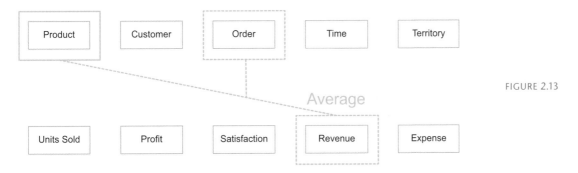

FIGURE 2.13

Here's the average revenue per product type per order, calculated as the mean:

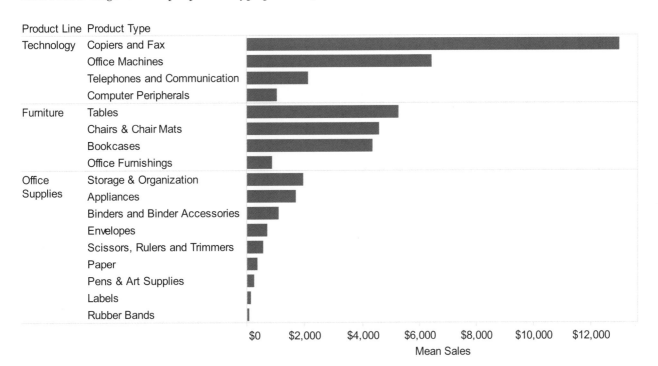

FIGURE 2.14

On average, two technology product types—Copiers and Fax as well as Office Machines—bring in more revenue per order than any other products

Notice that I haven't arranged items in alphabetical order but instead ranked them by value from highest to lowest. There is only one purpose for arranging items alphabetically: to make it easy to find a particular item in a long list. That isn't what we're doing here, however. Rather than looking up individual items, we are trying to see quantitative relationships within product lines and product types which is easiest to do when the product lines are arranged by value, either from high to low or low to high.

The current view lets us easily compare product types within product lines, but it would also be useful to compare product types without regard to product lines, which we can do by removing product lines from the view.

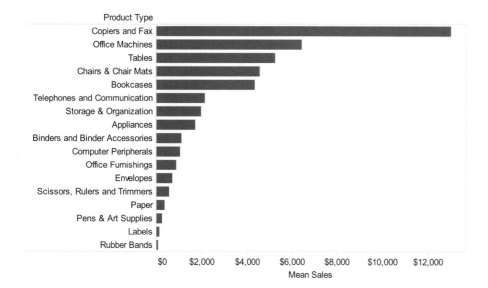

FIGURE 2.15

If we want to focus on average revenues of all product types without regard to product lines while maintaining an awareness of product lines, we can color-code the bars to distinguish them without changing the order. This strategy is illustrated below using green for technology, blue for furniture, and orange for office supplies.

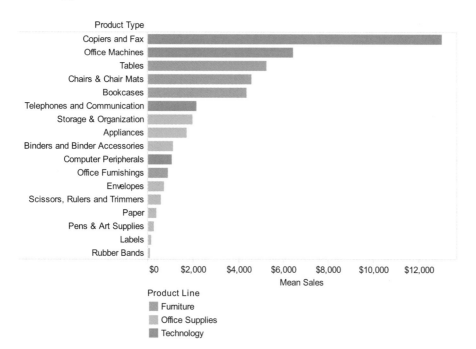

FIGURE 2.16

When we display values in ranked order, we can see how they are distributed across the entire set in addition to seeing how each item relates to the others. In the next chapter, we'll focus exclusively on the ways that values are distributed within particular measures. While examining variation within a category, as we're doing now, we can enrich our view of the distribution by dividing the ranked values into quartiles (four groups of 25% each), marking the median and the other boundaries between quartiles with vertical reference lines or bands of background color. In the example below, the vertical gray line marks the median, the left-hand edge of the gray-filled section marks the boundary between the first and second quartile, and its right-hand edge marks the boundary between the third and fourth quartiles.

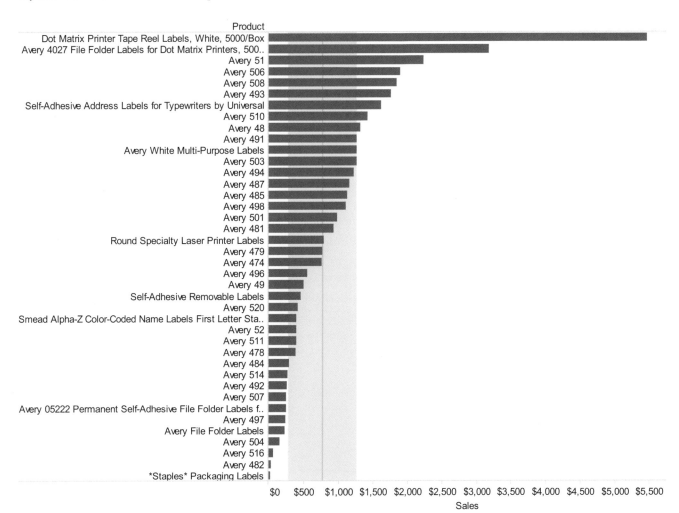

FIGURE 2.17

So far, we've examined only one measure at a time—a tally, sum, or mean—but it is often useful to see multiple measures at a time. We could do this by placing them side by side, as illustrated on the following page.

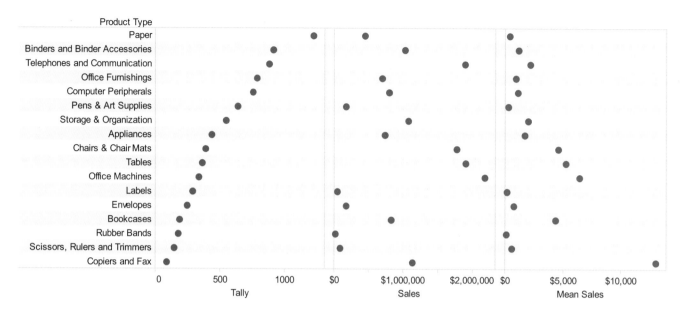

FIGURE 2.18

Another option, when we want to focus primarily on one measure but have an approximate sense of another measure available simultaneously, is to use color intensity to represent the secondary measure. In the example below, the length of each bar represents the sum of revenue for each product family, and the color intensity from light to dark represents the number of products sold within each family.

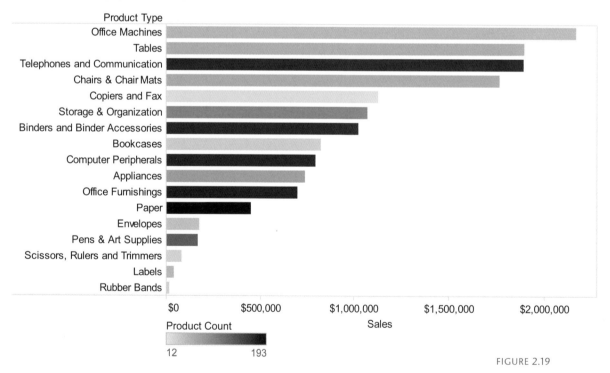

FIGURE 2.19

We could continue to explore products as we have been, fluidly shifting among tallies, sums, and means—sometimes looking at one at a time and sometimes looking at more than one—to build our understanding bit by bit. We won't exhaust the possibilities here in the book, but let's go just a little further

by moving down the hierarchy to the final level, product. We'll begin with a
tally.

Product Line	Product Type	Tally
Office Supplies	Paper	193
	Binders and Binder Accessories	134
	Pens & Art Supplies	101
	Storage & Organization	87
	Appliances	72
	Labels	40
	Envelopes	36
	Rubber Bands	30
	Scissors, Rulers and Trimmers	22
Technology	Telephones and Communication	126
	Computer Peripherals	97
	Office Machines	56
	Copiers and Fax	12
Furniture	Office Furnishings	134
	Chairs & Chair mats	51
	Tables	42
	Bookcases	30

FIGURE 2.20

To examine individual products, we must deal with a much longer list of items
than previously. A regular bar graph or dot plot could not display this number of
products on a computer screen without requiring us to scroll to see the entire
set. To see all of the products simultaneously, which is necessary to get a sense of
the whole, we can switch to a different type of visualization that can display
many more items at once on a screen: a *treemap*.

FIGURE 2.21

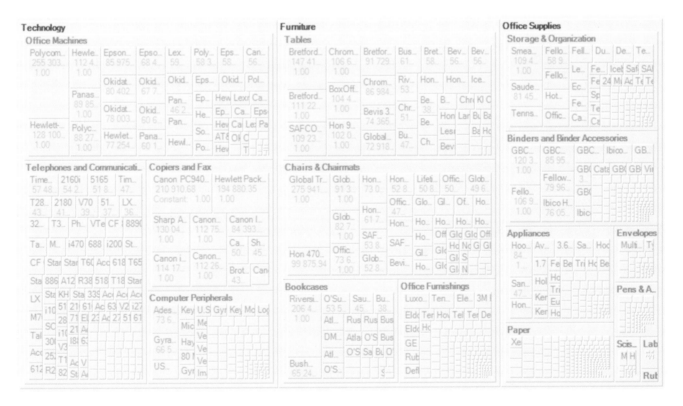

In this example, the sizes of individual rectangles represent product revenues, which have been organized into product types and product lines. A treemap uses containment—rectangles contained within larger rectangles—to represent a hierarchy of up to three levels at once (four levels, actually, if you consider the entire set of products of all types as the highest level).

We've had to give something up to view all of these values at once, haven't we? One problem is that most of the rectangles aren't large enough to display the product names. Even if this problem didn't exist, however, we would still be forced to compare the sizes of rectangles. Our brains are well designed for comparing the lengths of objects that share a common baseline (e.g., bars) or the positions of objects (e.g., dots), but our brains struggle to compare the sizes of rectangles in a treemap, handling this task with less precision. For ease and accuracy of comparison, it would be better to stick with a bar graph or dot plot. So why use a treemap if it increases perceptual difficulty and sacrifices precision? Because in this case we need to see and compare everything at once, which we can't do with a bar graph or dot plot simply because there isn't enough room on the screen. When viewing data, we must sometimes compromise our ability to do some things in order to increase our ability to do something else.

Treemaps were designed to display part-to-whole relationships. Similarly, pie charts are exclusively used to display parts of a whole. However, there is absolutely no reason to use a pie chart to explore and analyze data. A bar graph or dot plot with the values in ranked order is always more effective because our brains compare the lengths of bars with ease and precision whereas they cannot compare slices of a pie with comparable accuracy. Whenever we want to easily see the degree to which each value in a bar graph contributes to the whole, we can simply use a percentage scale on the quantitative axis, as shown below.

Ben Shneiderman originally created treemaps to visualize the contents of hard disks with tens of thousands of files in 5-15 levels of directories.

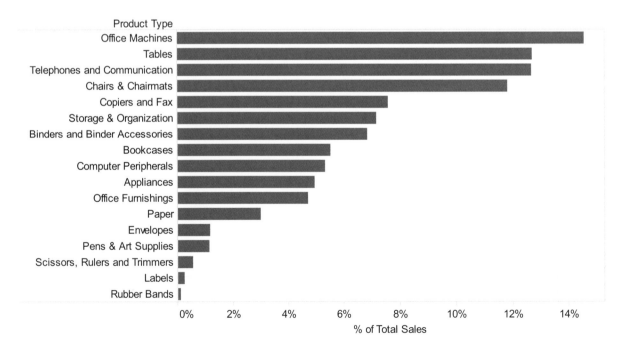

FIGURE 2.22

To enhance our view, in addition to product revenues represented by rectangle size, we can simultaneously use color intensity from light (least) to dark (most) to represent units sold, as illustrated below.

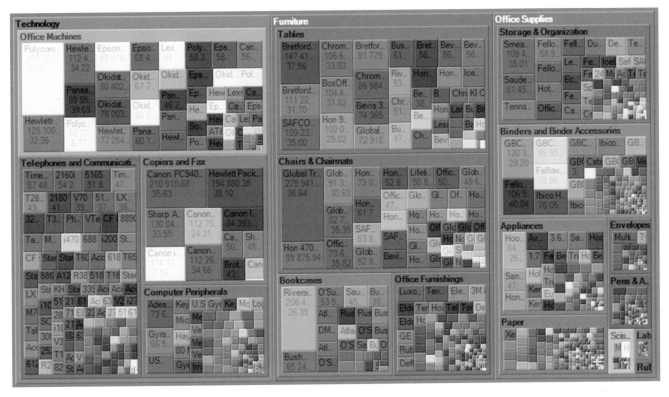

FIGURE 2.23

We began by using bar graphs and dot plots to examine ranking and part-to-whole relationships within categories, and we switched to treemaps when the number of values exceeded what a bar graph or dot plot could handle. A few other types of graphs also come in handy for examining variation within categories. We'll move on to those graphs in a moment. But first, a word about the importance of looking at data from multiple perspectives.

One of the fundamental principles of data analysis is that, to fully understand data, we must examine it from every possible perspective. It's fair to say that we never fully understand a set of data because we never manage to view it from every possible angle, so our understanding always resides somewhere along a continuum between complete uncertainty and complete certainty. As data analysts, we strive to reduce uncertainty. It's acceptable that we never achieve certainty. This limit to our knowledge keeps us humble and open to the possibility of being wrong. Besides, complete certainty isn't necessary. Increasingly better decisions can be made as uncertainty decreases. Where we reside along the continuum is a perpetual balancing act between reducing uncertainty to a useful level while not expending effort that could have been better used for other purposes. We maintain this balance as well as possible by always remaining focused on our goals and priorities.

The fact that we should examine data from many perspectives leads to another useful insight: no one view of the data will tell us everything. We explore and analyze data through a continuous and fluid process of shifting from one view to the next. Even though bar graphs and dot plots will serve as our primary means to view ranking and part-to-whole relationships within categories, with an occasional treemap thrown in for large sets of values, a few other visualizations will complete our toolset by serving specialized roles.

Specialized Graphs

Pareto Charts

Vilfredo Federico Damaso Pareto was an Italian engineer, economist, and sociologist who lived from 1848 to 1923. He is best known for his observation that several things (e.g., wealth) are often disproportionately associated with a small group of items (e.g., a small set of countries). This began with his initial observation that 80% of the property in Italy was owned by 20% of the people. We refer to distributions of this type as the *80/20 rule* or as exhibiting the *Pareto principle*.

Exploring these kinds of associations involves both of the quantitative relationships that we've been examining in this chapter: ranking and part-to-whole. We begin with a measure, such as household spending, associate it with a category, such as type of spending, and then arrange the categorical items (types of spending in this case) in ranked order from the one with the most to the one with the least.

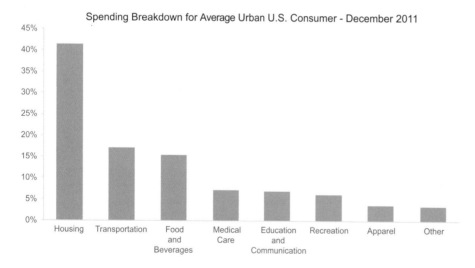

FIGURE 2.24

To view how these items contribute to the whole, we can add a line to the graph to show cumulative values, starting with the first item and continuing to the end where the cumulative total equals 100%.

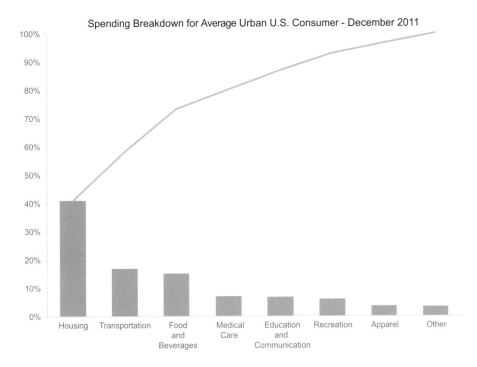

FIGURE 2.25

In honor of its originator, we call a graph of this type a *Pareto chart*. It is specifically designed to help us see how the parts of something, in ranked order from most to least, contribute to the whole of something in a way that can lead to insights such as the one in the annotation that appears in chart below.

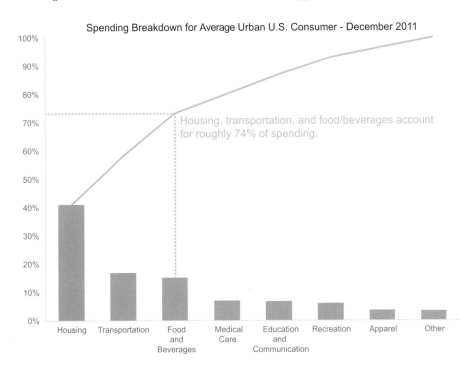

FIGURE 2.26

When we view the contributors to the whole in this manner, we can see that the top three spending categories constitute 74% of total expenditures.

If the category consists of a large number of items, such as many people, we can bin the items into percentile groups. For example, I once displayed sales orders in a Pareto chart that divided orders by size into groups of 10% each, which looked like this:

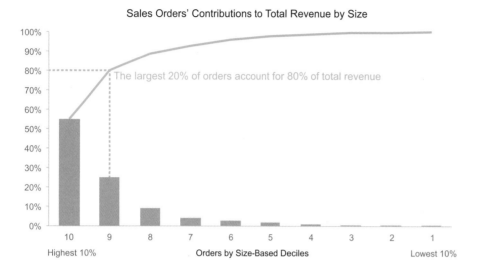

FIGURE 2.27

Part-to-whole relationships that exhibit disproportionate distributions such as this can contribute a great deal to our understanding of an organization.

Slope Graphs

A slope graph is nothing more than a line graph with values for only two points in time. Below is a simple example that shows how unemployment rates in all 50 U.S. states changed from 2012 to 2013.

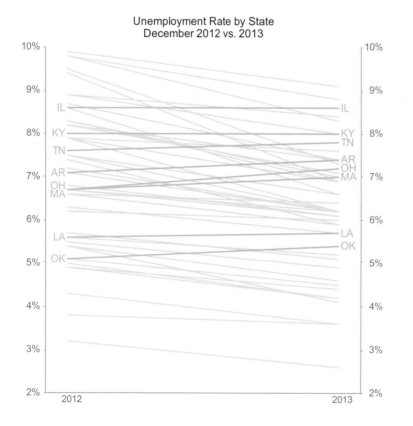

FIGURE 2.28

To eliminate clutter in this particular example, I've labeled only the states where the unemployment rate increased.

A slope graph makes it easy to focus on three features of change in time:

- Direction of change, indicated by an upward slope for increase and a downward slope for decrease
- Magnitude of change, indicated by the degree of the line's slope
- Changes in rank among categorical items, indicated by line intersections

If the quantitative scale on a slope graph represents percentages of the whole (i.e., out of 100%) for each categorical item at a particular point in time (see below), then the graph can also make it easy to see changes in part-to-whole relationships.

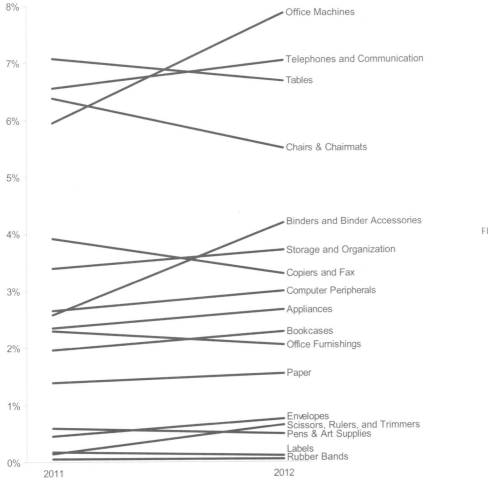

FIGURE 2.29

Most data analysis software does not include a chart type called a slope graph, but any product that supports line graphs should be able to produce slope graphs.

Deviation Bar Graphs

I call a bar graph that directly expresses differences in two sets of values, such as
the changes that occurred between two points in time, a *deviation bar graph*.
Deviation bar graphs are handy when we want to focus exclusively on the
amount or degree of change between two points in time without concern for
changes in ranking or part-to-whole relationships. These graphs can take the
form of simple bar graphs that express the information directly as either positive
or negative values, which are easy to read and compare, illustrated below on the
right.

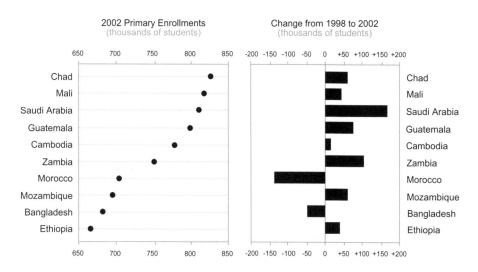

FIGURE 2.30

Funnel Plots

Occasionally, items in a category require adjustments before fair comparisons
can be made among them because particular factors can influence some items in
a category differently than others. This can produce misleading variation in the
values that we're comparing. For example, if we want to compare scholastic
performance of students who come from both low-income and high-income
households, we should first determine whether household income affects
student performance, and, if so, to what extent. Then we should adjust the
measures of student performance to account for this factor before we compare
the students. If we fail to do this, our comparison will be thrown off by the
effects of poverty and affluence, and we won't actually see how the abilities of
the students themselves differ, all else being equal. We refer to this adjustment
process as *standardizing* data.

   Adjusting for inflation is another example of standardization to account for
factors that would otherwise skew comparisons. The fact that gasoline doubled
in price during a particular period of time means something quite different than
it seems if the purchasing power of the dollar was halved during that period.

   Another difference that we must sometimes take into account is variation in
the sizes of the samples that we're comparing. The adjustment that's needed in
this case can be handled graphically, in the form of a special version of a scatter

plot called a *funnel plot*. Funnel plots address the fact that categorical items that contain relatively few instances of the thing being measured exhibit a greater degree of random variation when compared to categorical items with many instances. This must be taken into account when comparing the two. A little later, we'll take a look at this problem in relation to healthcare data, and we'll see the solution that funnel plots offer. But first, let's get more familiar with the effects of sample size on randomness.

Consider the following display, called a *caterpillar plot*, of healthcare data. Each of the 260 data points represents a hospital. The values are mortality rates following surgeries. The solid horizontal lines represent the mean.

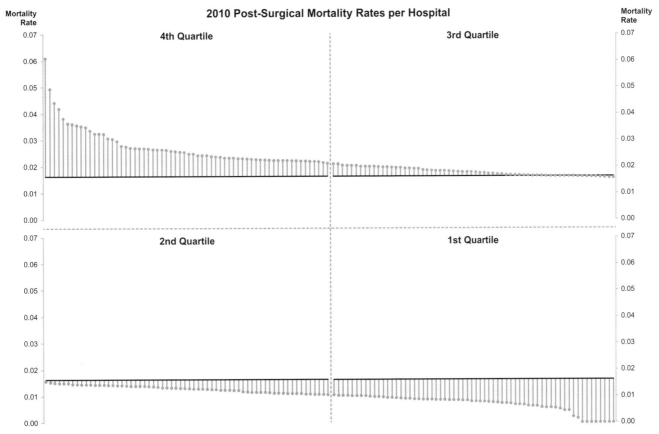

FIGURE 2.31

The numbers of surgeries reported by each hospital on which this graph is based range from 7 to 3,151. Because of the wide variation in numbers of surgeries reported by each hospital, we do not get accurate comparative information when we rank the hospitals by mortality rate. That is, the ranking suggests a relationship of relative performance that cannot be determined from the data.

Imagine that, unlike the anonymous version of the graph above, each data point is labeled with the hospital's name. Can you hear the objections of surgeons from the hospitals with the highest mortality rates in the 4th quartile section of the chart? Can you imagine the unjustified pride of the surgeons who work at the hospitals with mortality rates of zero in the 1st quartile section? One of the hospitals with a zero mortality rate provided a sample of only seven surgeries, not enough on which to base any conclusions or allow an accurate comparison to another hospital that reported thousands of surgeries.

The funnel plot was first introduced by R. J. Light and D. B. Pillemer in 1984. It is nothing more than a scatter plot that displays measures of something (e.g., post-surgical mortality rates) associated with categorical items (e.g., hospitals) along the Y axis and sample sizes (e.g., the number of surgeries per hospital) along the X axis, with a data point for each item and lines to mark the boundaries of random variation. These boundary lines start out far apart from each other on the left where the numbers of instances are small and converge as they proceed to the right where the numbers of instances are large. In other words, the lines mark broader boundaries of random variation for small samples and increasingly restrictive boundaries as sample sizes grow. This gives the boundary lines the shape of a funnel.

Funnel plots strive to distinguish random from non-random variation in distributions much as statistical process control charts do for time-series, which we'll learn about in *Chapter 9 – Install Signal Sensors*. Typically, a funnel plot includes two sets of boundary lines: one set for 95% confidence intervals (calculated as standard error × 1.96), which statistical process control calls a two-sigma limit, and one for 99.8% confidence intervals (calculated as standard error × 3), called a three-sigma limit. Here's how a funnel plot might look without data:

R. J. Light and D. B. Pillemer (1984). *Summing Up: The Science of Reviewing Research*. Harvard University Press.

Standard error is the measure of how much random variation we would expect from samples of equal size drawn from the same population. In other words, if you constructed several random samples of the same size and determined the mean of each (sampling distribution of the mean), the standard error would be the standard deviation of that distribution of means. Standard error can be applied to any statistics, not just the mean. Knowing how much error you can expect when selecting a sample of a given size from a population helps you determine if your sample is meaningfully different from the population

FIGURE 2.32

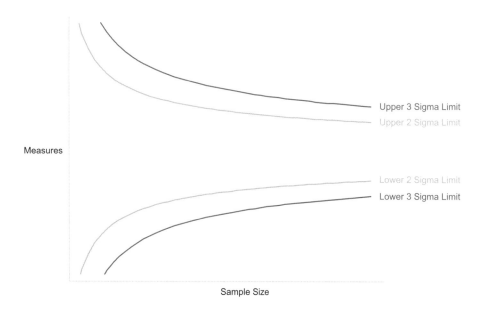

When the plot is populated with values, each data point that falls outside of the range defined within the upper and lower two-sigma limits would represent a value that would only be due to randomness 5% of the time. Any point that falls outside the three-sigma limits would be due to randomness extremely rarely— approximately 0.2% of the time.

Before we populate a funnel plot with the post-surgical mortality data described above, let's look at a simpler example. Imagine that we're examining 10 salespeople to see how successful they've been in converting sales opportunities into actual sales, but the opportunities that the salespeople were given varied significantly: three salespeople were given only 2 opportunities each, and the others were given from 10 to 1,000 each. Under these circumstances, would it be appropriate to compare their performance in the following manner?

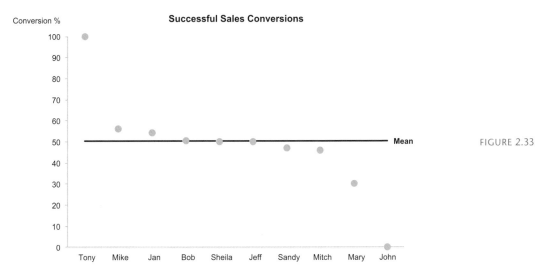

FIGURE 2.33

This isn't a fair comparison. Tony's 100% conversion rate and John's 0% conversion rate were both based on only two opportunities each. Mike's 56% conversion rate indicates that he failed 44% of the time, which means 176 failures out of 400 opportunities. For all we know, Mike might have failed on each of his first 20 attempts, so is he necessarily more successful than John? No. Yet graphs of data like this are often used to make judgments such as the ones indicated in the colored bands in the version below:

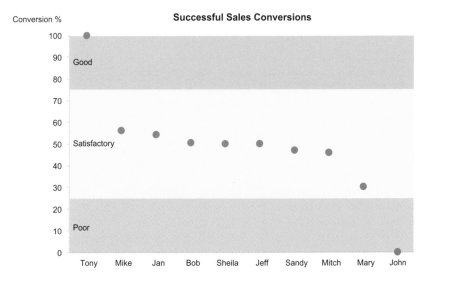

FIGURE 2.34

Assigning ranges of acceptable variation either arbitrarily or based on a statistical measure such as the mean without taking wide-ranging sample sizes into account assigns unjustified significance to data. The nature of random variation must be considered. Here's a funnel plot of the same data:

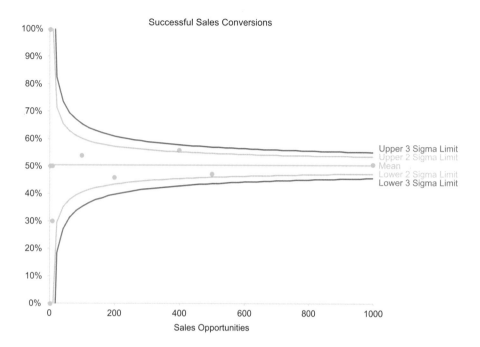

FIGURE 2.35

Now that the varying numbers of sales opportunities have been taken into account, we can see that no sales representative had a sales conversion rate that fell outside the range of variation that might be entirely due to randomness.

Now let's look at the post-surgical mortality rates from before. Unfortunately, we can't just throw the mortality rates that appeared in the earlier chart into a funnel without first doing a little work. Funnel plots calculate the boundaries of expected variation based on the mean and standard error, but the mean as a measure of center and standard errors as measures of confidence around the mean are statistics that assume a normal (bell-shaped) distribution. Here's what the distribution of mortality rates looks like when displayed in a histogram:

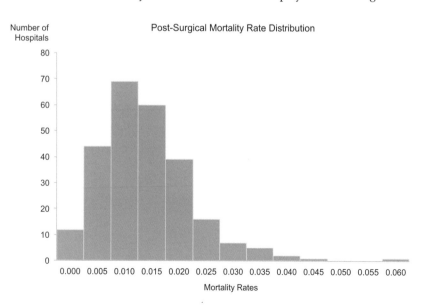

FIGURE 2.36

This distribution is skewed to the higher values on the right (skew is determined by the direction of the tail of the distribution's shape, not the peak). The peak is on the left. The mean and standard error will not describe the nature of this distribution in a way that will allow us to calculate meaningful boundaries of random variation. This doesn't mean that we can't use a funnel plot, however. Statisticians routinely use statistics that assume a normal distribution to work with data that does not exhibit a normal shape. They do this by first transforming the values to produce a normally shaped distribution. A typical way to do this when dealing with a distribution that is slightly skewed toward the high values involves a square root transformation (a.k.a., square root transform). I've taken the liberty of transforming the surgery mortality rates using Excel's SQRT() function, which results in the following distribution:

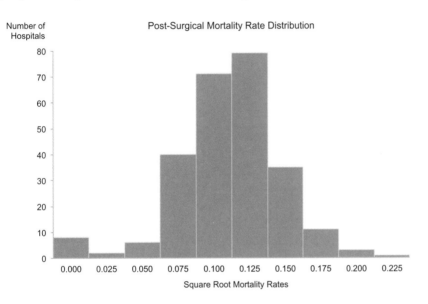

FIGURE 2.37

Now that we have a fairly normal distribution shape, we can display these post-surgical mortality rates in a funnel plot.

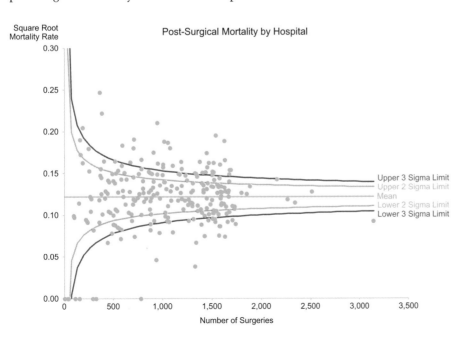

FIGURE 2.38

This funnel plot displays one data point per hospital. Each data point shows the number of surgeries and the square-root-transformed mortality rate. The square roots of the mortality rates are not particularly meaningful in and of themselves, but that doesn't matter because we're simply trying to identify the hospitals that exhibit a level of performance that is outside of the boundaries of random variation and that is, therefore (using the language of statistical process control) probably due to a "special cause." The farther a value falls outside of the boundaries, the more likely it is the result of a special cause rather than of randomness.

Notice in the lower left-hand corner of the same plot below that two of the hospitals with mortality rates of zero reside within the boundaries, which indicates that we cannot rely on their low rates as significant.

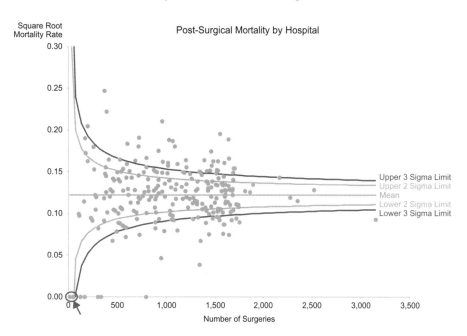

FIGURE 2.39

In making this comparison, we're assuming that the hospitals are homogeneous, all part of a single system, that is, that there are no external variables such as policies regarding surgeon work hours or rationales for undertaking surgery that we have to take into account before comparing the mortality rates. By adjusting for the varying numbers of surgeries performed at these hospitals, we are hoping to answer the question, "How is this system of hospitals doing in its efforts to prevent post-surgical mortalities?" No longer are we encouraged to compare hospital performance as a misleading ranking. We are now encouraged to focus exclusively on signals in the data. Unfortunately, however, we have not yet met our objective of comparing post-surgical mortality rates within a homogeneous system. That is, we have not adjusted the mortality rates to account for two factors that still prevent the hospitals from being a homogeneous system:

1. Surgeries of many types are being compared without taking into account that different surgeries vary significantly in their mortality risk.
2. Patients of varying health are being compared without taking into account that some went into surgery much healthier than others and were therefore at less risk of dying.

We could solve these problems by making further adjustments to standardize the data, but for now we have seen the utility of funnel plots for establishing the boundaries of random variation, so we won't venture into more detail about this particular data set.

Funnel plots can be used for many types of data. For example, we might want to compare the profit margins of similar products, some of which sell few units and some of which sell many, so that we can identify products with significantly low and high margins. Because differences in sample size (the number of units sold for each product) will have an effect on random variation, a funnel plot might handle this question well. Once we know how to calculate the boundaries of random variation (the two- and three-sigma limits), funnel plots are relatively easy to construct in several charting products, including Excel. As I mentioned previously, a funnel plot is essentially a scatter plot designed for a specific purpose.

If you really want to dig into funnel plots more deeply, some excellent resources can be found at the website www.understandinguncertainty.org, which features the work of David Spiegelhalter, a professor of statistics at the University of Cambridge.

So far, we've held the categories of space and time in reserve to consider later. Before we move on to them, it will help us to become familiar with variation within measures, which is where we're heading in the next chapter.

To show how to construct a funnel plot in Excel, including the formulas that are required to calculate the boundary lines, I created an Excel file that you can download. It contains everything that you'll ordinarily need, including instructions. You can copy your own data into this Excel file, and, by following a few simple steps, produce a funnel plot. Keep in mind, however, that this particular template only works for proportions (rates from 0 through 1 or percentages from 0% through 100%). You can download the file at: www.perceptualedge.com/signal/funnel_plot_template.xlsx

One of the downsides of producing funnel plots in Excel is that this product doesn't allow us to attach labels to data points in scatter plots. This is a glaring omission because it's so often necessary to be able to easily identify individual data points in a scatter plot. For this reason, when we hover with the mouse over a particular data point in our Excel file, only the quantitative values appear, not the name of the hospital. Fortunately, to overcome this problem, we can download a free Excel add-in called Chart Labeler at www.appspro.com/Utilities/ChartLabeler.htm

3 VARIATION WITHIN MEASURES

When we examine variation within measures, we're interested in distribution relationships: the ways in which the values are distributed across the quantitative range. Important stories reside in distributions. Fortunately, they're relatively easy to see. We'll rely a bit on statistics, but mostly we'll be using our eyes.

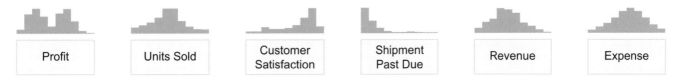

FIGURE 3.1

Examining variation within a measure fits our metaphor of surveying the land especially well because a visual representation of a quantitative distribution can look a lot like a landscape.

FIGURE 3.2

When we view this graph, it isn't hard to imagine that we're looking at a mountain range in the distance, with a prominent peak near the center and foothills on both sides. Because this is a familiar sight, upon which humans have gazed in awe for eons, it's easy for us to perceive a distribution of values when it's displayed in this way.

Distribution Relationships

Many data analysts have never examined the distribution of a measure's values other than a simple average. However, an average, which measures the center of a distribution, is not enough information in most cases. Consider a company that pays its employees a mean salary of $55,000 per year. What does this mean salary figure tell us about the distribution of salaries? Are most employees paid salaries that are close to $55,000? Are some employees paid a whole lot more than others? The mean won't tell us.

When we talk about an average or typical value in a set, we're talking about what statisticians call the *central tendency*. This is a single value that summarizes an entire set by locating its center. In addition to the central tendency of the salaries above, we should also know the full range across which the salaries are distributed, from the lowest to the highest. This is called the *spread* of the distribution. In this particular example, salaries roughly range from $21,000 to $110,000, a spread of $89,000.

In addition to the central tendency and spread, there is one more characteristic that we must know if we are to have a good sense of a distribution. Do you know what that additional characteristic is? Perhaps it will help if I show a picture of a salary distribution.

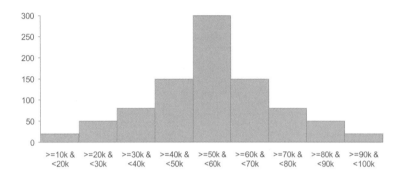

FIGURE 3.3

What can we now see in addition to the central tendency and spread? The third characteristic is the *shape* of the distribution. This particular distribution is bell-shaped, also called a *normal distribution*. Until we saw this graph, we had no idea how the salaries were distributed across the spread. Knowing that the mean is $55,000 and that the spread ranges from $21,000 to $110,000 told us nothing certain about the distribution's shape. To demonstrate this, here's another distribution of salaries with the same central tendency and spread, but a very different shape.

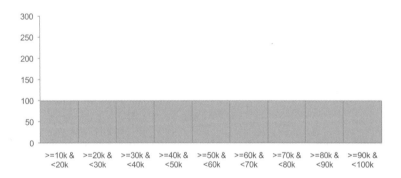

FIGURE 3.4

This is a *uniform distribution*. The salaries are evenly distributed across the entire range. Salaries with the same central tendency and spread could also be distributed as shown in this next example:

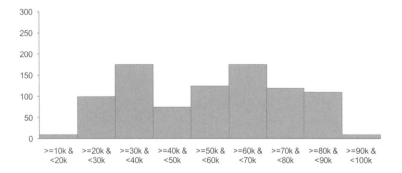

FIGURE 3.5

This is called a bi-peaked, or more formally, a *bimodal distribution*, because it has two prominent peaks.

Are you getting the picture? Until we know the shape of a distribution, we know relatively little about it. Important stories reside in the shape.

I want to drive home the importance of this by making it personal. Imagine that you had some medical tests a week ago, and you're now sitting in the doctor's office waiting for the results. The doctor clears her throat a little awkwardly and says, "I'm sorry to inform you that you have an incurable form of cancer called abdominal mesothelioma." Your body grows rigid as you struggle with the implications. Cancer! Not just cancer, but an incurable form of cancer. Once you gain some control over the fear, you ask the inevitable question, "Doctor, how long do I have to live?" Even more awkwardly than before, the doctor replies, "On average, people in your situation live for eight months." Eight months! You've just been told that you have only eight more months to live! But wait a minute. Was that actually what the doctor said? No, what she said was that "on average" people live for eight months. She just gave you a measure of central tendency.

After getting over your initial shock and recovering some control of your thoughts, you ask the doctor about the range of time people can potentially survive this cancer. She responds, "Some people die almost immediately and some go on to live for as many as 20 more years." Wow, that's a huge spread. If people survive only eight months on average but can live for as much as 20 more years, the distribution of survival is highly skewed with an early peak and then a long tail that stretches far into the future.

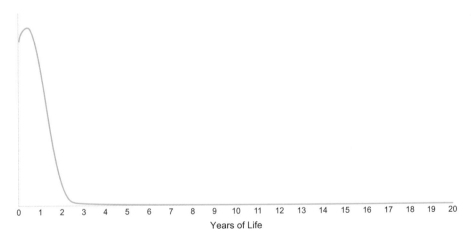

Years of Life

FIGURE 3.6

You now know the central tendency, the spread, and a rough sense of the shape of this distribution. At this point, you would probably rush back home to log onto your computer and research this form of cancer to find out about the people who usually to live the longest, hoping that you're lot like them.

This morbid scenario that I've asked you to imagine was more than a thought experiment for the respected Harvard evolutionary biologist Stephen J. Gould back in the early 1980s when he was diagnosed with abdominal mesothelioma. What you've just imagined was very real for him. As a scientist who worked with data and was trained in statistics, he understood the importance of investigating distributions beyond simple measures of center. He wrote about his experience in an article entitled "The Median Isn't the Message." Here's some of what he wrote:

> *We still carry the historical baggage of a Platonic heritage that seeks sharp essences and definite boundaries…This Platonic heritage, with its emphasis in clear distinctions and separated immutable entities, leads us to view statistical measures of central tendency wrongly, indeed opposite to the appropriate interpretation in our actual world of variation, shadings, and continua. In short, we view means and medians as the hard "realities," and the variation that permits their calculation as a set of transient and imperfect measurements of this hidden essence. If the median is the reality and variation around the median just a device for its calculation, then "I will probably be dead in eight months" may pass as a reasonable interpretation.*
>
> *Variation itself is nature's only irreducible essence. Variation is the hard reality, not a set of imperfect measures for a central tendency. Means and medians are the abstractions.*

The story of Stephen Jay Gould's experience with cancer statistics was found in the *CancerGuide*, created and maintained by Steve Dunn, at www.cancerguide.org.

Gould went on to live for 20 more years and did some of his best work near the end. As a scientist, Gould didn't need to face death to appreciate the importance of variation in distributions. Most of us lack the training and experience that instilled this appreciation in him. Knowing that variation in distributions can reveal life-and-death stories helps to drive their importance home.

Normal Distributions

A normal distribution is one that's symmetrically shaped with a peak in the center and similar declines on both sides of that peak.

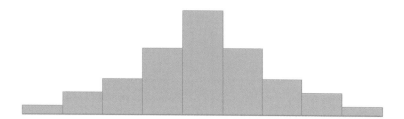

FIGURE 3.7

The term "normal" might suggest that a distribution of this particular shape is routine, proper, or desired. This is not necessarily the case. A normal distribution is significant for the following reasons:

- No other distribution shape occurs more frequently in nature.
- It describes the distribution of random error.
- It is particularly useful for *predictive statistics* (i.e., predicting what might happen based on what's happened in the past).

The normal distribution was first noticed by scientists in the 19th century who were excitedly studying newly available social data and observed unexpected regularity in the patterns of distribution. That is, a great deal of variation in social data that appeared to be random at the level of individual values exhibited a bell-shaped distribution at the aggregate level. Leonard Mlodinow describes this discovery in the following paragraph:

> *We associate randomness with disorder. Yet although the lives of 200 million drivers vary unforeseeably, in the aggregate their behavior could hardly have proved more orderly. Analogous regularities can be found if we examine how people vote, buy stocks, marry, are told to get lost, misaddress letters, or sit in traffic on their way to a meeting they didn't want to go to in the first place—or if we measure the length of their legs, the size of their feet, the width of their buttocks, or the breadth of their beer bellies. As nineteenth-century scientists dug into newly available social data, wherever they looked, the chaos of life seemed to produce quantifiable and predictable patterns. But it was not just the regularities that astonished them. It was also the nature of the variation. Social data, they discovered, often follow the normal distribution.*

Leonard Mlodinow (2008). *The Drunkard's Walk: How Randomness Rules Our Lives.* Pantheon Books, page 148.

Some of these scientists became excited by the prevalence of bell-shaped distributions and assumed that they were more common than they actually are. Although bell-shaped distributions are prevalent, distributions come in many shapes. For example, in the financial realm, distributions are often far from bell-shaped.

> *If film revenue were normally distributed, most films would earn near some average amount, and two-thirds of all film revenue would fall within a standard deviation from that number. But in the film business, 20 percent of the movies bring in 80 percent of the revenue. Such hit-driven businesses, though thoroughly unpredictable, follow a far different distribution, one for which the concepts of mean and standard deviation have no meaning because there is no "typical" performance, and megahit outliers, which in an ordinary business might occur only once every few centuries, happen every few years.*

Ibid., page 160.

Random errors in measurement at the aggregate level routinely exhibit normal distributions. Measurements vary because humans and our instruments are imperfect, but this variation is predictable, with values both above and below the mean that tend to balance one another out. Errors in performance often exhibit this pattern. When a skilled archer aims for the bulls-eye on a target, the degree to which he misses the mark over a series of shots forms a normal distribution. In old English, for an archer to miss the mark was to "sin," a term that remains familiar today because of its frequent use in the Bible, beginning with the King James version. The better the archer, the tighter the dispersion of his sins will be, but the shape of the distribution as a whole will be normal if more than a few arrows have been shot.

We'll be sticking with *descriptive statistics* throughout this book (descriptions of what is), never venturing into *predictive statistics*, so the predictive benefits of normal distributions won't concern us. When we encounter normal distributions, we'll take advantage of the fact that values are dispersed around the mean

We're avoiding predictive statistics, not because they aren't useful, but merely because they lie outside the scope of this book. Signals reside in data about things that actually happened. We try to detect, understand, and track signals to maintain good performance or to improve performance. Predicting what might happen based on probabilities that we've observed in historical data is incredibly useful because it potentially enables us to create the future that we desire or to at least make an informed attempt. However, these kinds of predictive statistics involve more advanced concepts and practices than the ones that we're using in this book. We'll reserve our attempts to shape the future for a future book.

in a specific manner. As illustrated below, in a normal distribution, based on a known mean and standard deviation, we always know the quantitative ranges within which 68%, 95%, and 99.7% of the values fall.

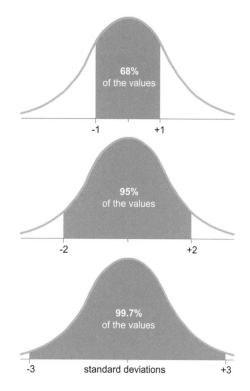

FIGURE 3.8

Knowing these quantitative ranges can at times be useful in descriptive statistics but is even more useful when testing hypotheses and predicting future outcomes under specific conditions. What's critical is that we observe the actual shape of a distribution, normal or not, and figure out what that shape reveals about the measure.

If we roll two dice at a craps table in a casino, the probabilities of each possible sum exhibit the shape of a normal distribution. Each die can have a value of 1 through 6, producing 36 (6 × 6) possible combinations when two dice are rolled, resulting in 12 possible sums. Some sums have a greater chance of coming up than others because there are more ways to achieve them. The probability of a particular sum depends on the number of ways it can occur. Here are all 36 combinations of values and their sums:

36 Possible Combinations of Dice Values

	1	2	3	4	5	6	7	8	9	10	11	12	13	14	15	16	17	18	19	20	21	22	23	24	25	26	27	28	29	30	31	32	33	34	35	36
Die #1	1	1	1	1	1	1	2	2	2	2	2	2	3	3	3	3	3	3	4	4	4	4	4	4	5	5	5	5	5	5	6	6	6	6	6	6
Die #2	1	2	3	4	5	6	1	2	3	4	5	6	1	2	3	4	5	6	1	2	3	4	5	6	1	2	3	4	5	6	1	2	3	4	5	6
Sums	2	3	4	5	6	7	3	4	5	6	7	8	4	5	6	7	8	9	5	6	7	8	9	10	6	7	8	9	10	11	7	8	9	10	11	12

FIGURE 3.9

Only one combination of values produces a sum of 2 (1+1) and only one produces a sum of 12 (6+6). Two combinations sum to 3 (1+2 and 2+1), three sum to 4 (1+3, 2+2, 3+1), and so on up to 7, the sum with the highest probability because it can be achieved through six combinations (1+6, 2+5, 3+4, 4+3, 5+2, 6+1). Here's a graph of the frequency distribution of all possible sums, which perfectly exhibits the shape of a normal distribution.

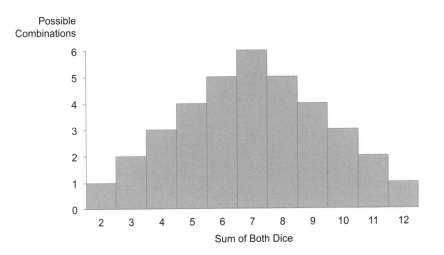

FIGURE 3.10

What is the probability that the two dice will total 3? The answer is 2 out of 36: a 5.5% probability (5 ÷ 36 = 0.055). The shape of the probabilities associated with the outcomes of a particular event, such as rolling dice, is known as that event's *probability distribution*. If the shape of a particular probability distribution is normal, even though the roll of each individual die is entirely subject to chance and completely unpredictable, the sums of two dice rolled many times will, in the aggregate, exhibit a normal distribution. This is predictable based on known probabilities. Because we have examined the frequency distribution of possible outcomes, this should be easy to understand. We wouldn't expect it to work in any other way. If we roll the dice 100 times and record the outcomes, the distribution might not perfectly match a normal shape, but it will come very close. If we do this several times, each set of 100 rolls will likely exhibit a slightly different distribution shape but always close to normal. Furthermore, if we recorded any statistic related to 100 rolls of the dice, such as the mean, and we did it over and over, the shape of the distribution of that statistic would be normal as well.

The more times we roll the dice, the closer the distribution of the sums will fit the shape of a normal curve. Because the probability of each possible outcome is known, the shape of the distribution of the sums of two dice in the aggregate is also known. If we had to bet our lives on the outcome of a particular roll, we'd be dumb to bet on anything other than 7 because 7 has the highest probability.

So, even though there is a great deal of randomness at the level of individual observations (e.g., each roll of a single die), there is a great deal of order in the aggregate. Each die coming up with a value from 1 through 6 is completely random—equally possible—but the possible sums of the numbers on both dice are not equally possible, and can therefore be predicted.

When we roll a single die over and over, because each possible value from 1 through 6 has an equal chance of coming up (assuming the die is properly weighted), this random probability results in a uniform distribution of values, illustrated below.

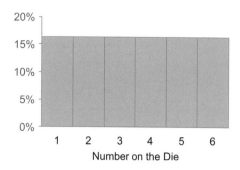

FIGURE 3.11

The normal distribution of many rolls of two dice is relatively easy to understand, but many phenomena that we measure in the real world with normal distributions are harder to understand. Consider measures of intelligence in the form of *intelligence quotient (IQ)*. The shape of IQ distribution in the population as a whole is normal. The measurement scale was originally devised such that the mean IQ had a score of 100. If we measure the IQs of any randomly selected group of 100 people, the distribution of their IQs will be normal. By "randomly selected," I mean that everyone in the population has an equal chance of being selected, resulting in a *random sample*—one that is not influenced by any factor that would bias it in some way, such as exclusively selecting college students. If the distribution is skewed instead of normal, we would immediately know that our sample was not random and therefore not representative of the overall population.

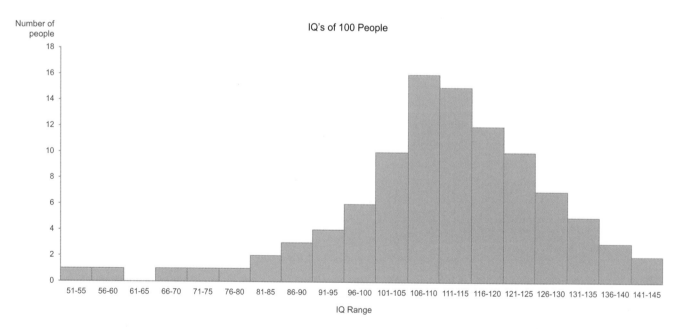

This is one of the ways that we discover factors that influence particular measures. Finding an abnormal distribution in a set of values that we expect to look normal clues us in to the fact that something other than randomness influenced the outcomes. Identifying that factor (e.g., discovering that the sample IQs were

FIGURE 3.12

collected from a small neighborhood with an unusually large number of professionals and academics) could lead to useful knowledge and steps to correct a problem.

The Nature of Randomness

Randomness is confusing even though it is intimately woven into the fabric of our lives.

> *The outline of our lives, like the candle's flame, is continuously coaxed in new directions by a variety of random events that, along with our responses to them, determine our fate. As a result, life is both hard to predict and hard to interpret.*

Leonard Mlodinow (2008). *The Drunkard's Walk: How Randomness Rules Our Lives.* Pantheon Books, page 4.

Randomness is a difficult concept that only makes sense after a great deal of thought. Perhaps this difficulty stems, in part, from our natural desire to feel in control. To accept randomness is to accept the fact that much in our lives just happens and remains forever beyond our control. The concept of randomness is existentially uncomfortable.

When considered in the context of probabilities, something is truly random if every possible outcome has an equal chance of occurring. This is what we mean by random chance. In this sense, an event is random if no information is available that would enable us to predict its outcome. For example, if a single die is properly weighted, there is no information that would help us predict the outcome of the next roll. The fact that the last three rolls in a row came up with a value of 6 tells us nothing about the roll to come. A value of 6 always has exactly the same one-in-six chance of occurring as the values 1 through 5.

Apart from the context of probability, we also use the term "randomness" to describe something else. We call variation in a measure random if we cannot discern a meaningful and predictable pattern in it. We shouldn't mistake randomness of this type for something meaningful, attribute it to a known cause, and waste time trying to fix it. Random variation has no recognizable cause; it simply *is*. In other words, measures tend to vary somewhat without an identifiable reason. But variation that simply *is*, without a cause, unless all probable outcomes are equal, doesn't seem to make sense, does it? Other than events such as the roll of a single die, how can something just happen, without a cause? In fact, most things don't just happen.

Consider your body temperature. You probably learned as a child that body temperature is normally 98.6 degrees Fahrenheit. Actually, body temperature differs somewhat depending on where the measurement is taken (mouth, skin, and other body parts that I won't mention) and the time of day, plus the norm differs a little from one person to another as well. But 98.6 is the mean. If you measured your temperature orally upon rising each morning for an entire month, you would find that it varies slightly to both sides of 98.6 (or around your own mean temperature, which might be slightly different) in the shape of a normal distribution. This qualifies as random variation, but does it really lack a cause? No, but it lacks a cause that we can identify, explain, and control. The cause is too subtle, perhaps too complex, entailing the interplay of multiple factors. What we call random variation is usually quite small and predictable, only rarely popping out in extremes, so we choose to accept it without concern. After all, what's the point of worrying if there's nothing we can do about it? It is nevertheless possible that, as our ability to understand previously mysterious phenomena improves, once in awhile something that was once considered random becomes better understood and attributed to a known cause, and therefore subject to control. Until then, however, we won't spend our time fretting over what we now experience as random; instead, we'll concentrate on variation with attributable causes that are within our reach and worth pursuing.

Non-Normal Distributions

When we measure things that exhibit variation that isn't random—variation that is caused by one or more factors that we can identify and potentially control—their distributions are often non-bell-shaped. Each of the following shapes exhibits something other than random variation.

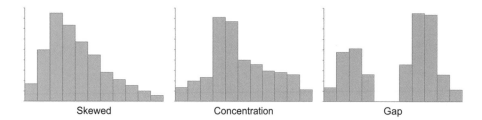

FIGURE 3.13

When a single peak resides closer to one side of the spread than the other, producing a skewed distribution, something is causing this to occur. The same is true of every shape illustrated above and of many other distribution shapes. This does not necessarily hold true if we're looking at small data sets, however, because in those sets there might not be enough values to reveal the true shape. For example, the distribution below of people by age exhibits a gap: it includes no people in their 30s or 40s.

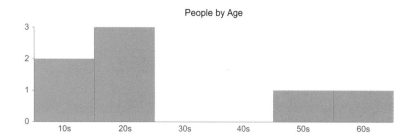

FIGURE 3.14

Ordinarily, this should arouse our curiosity, but once we know that there are only eight people in this set, we realize that the gap in ages would probably be filled in if the set were larger.

Distribution shapes are meaningful, and it's up to us to discover those meanings. For instance, medical research tends to produce data sets that are highly skewed. There is a reason for this. According to Andrew Vickers:

The simple explanation for what is going on here is that medical research typically involves studying patients with some kind of disease. By definition, these populations are not normal; they have presented for treatment exactly because they have something wrong...You hardly ever see normal distributions in medicine because you hardly ever study the "normal" population as a whole, only unusual subsets.

Andrew Vickers (2010). *What is a p-value anyway?* Addison-Wesley, pages 34-35.

Sometimes a distribution exhibits an abrupt beginning or end, such as the following example of people who join the military, distributed by age.

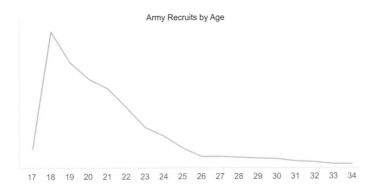

FIGURE 3.15

Shapes of this type usually indicate the existence of some condition that prevents values above or below a particular point, such as the requirement that a person be at least 17 years old to join the military with parental consent or 18 without it.

The distribution below is bimodel. This is not a small set of values, so something must be causing this bimodal shape. Can you think of a possible cause for this shape?

FIGURE 3.16

How about the distribution of salaries in an organization that has a large number of part-time employees? The lower peak could reflect typical part-time salaries and the higher peak typical full-time salaries. If the peaks were closer together, this could represent the heights of people in a group of women and men, with a lower peak for women and a higher peak for men. The photograph below illustrates this phenomenon with women in white and men in black.

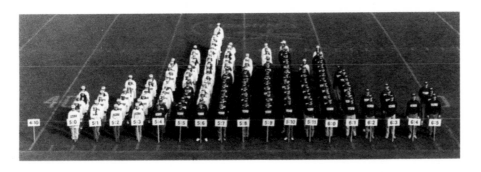

FIGURE 3.17: Mark F. Schilling, Ann E. Watkins, and William Watkins (August 2002). "Is Human Height Bimodal?" The American Statistician, No. 3, page 226.

The pattern stands out more clearly when visualized using stacked bars to show the totals per height as well as the male and female components.

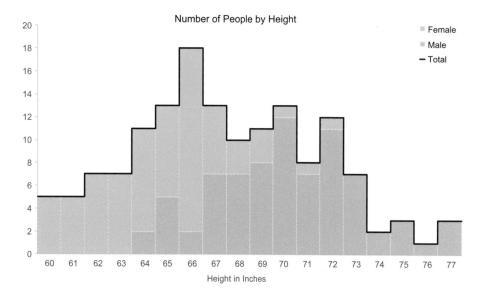

FIGURE 3.18

The following graph of the same data, with separate lines for males, females, and people in total, makes it easier to see the distribution of male and female heights individually:

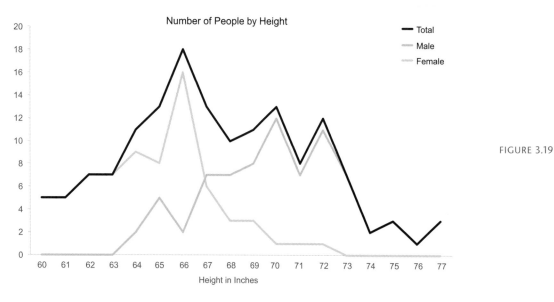

FIGURE 3.19

Notice that the black line sits on top of the pink or blue lines when either females or males make up the entire sample for particular heights, such as in the 60- to 63-inch range.

As we spend time examining variation within measures, we begin to recognize patterns that are meaningful when we encounter them in our own data. In time, with enough experience, we begin to recognize these patterns intuitively.

Homogeneity and Heterogeneity

The distribution of people's heights on the previous page was bimodal because it was heterogeneous, consisting of two significantly different groups: women and men. Multiple peaks are often the result of heterogeneity: the presence of discrete groups. In this case, if we examined the distributions of women's and men's heights separately, each would then consist of a homogeneous set of values, and each would be normal in shape.

Assuming homogeneity in a data set can lead to confusion about variation. What's causing these unusual peaks and troughs? The cause is often heterogeneity. One way to test for the source of heterogeneity that's responsible for unusual variation is to quickly break the data into multiple frequency distributions, one for each item in a relevant category. By doing this with the data set of heights above for the category of sex (male or female), switching from a single bimodal distribution to two normal distributions would have immediately revealed that sex was the responsible for the bi-modal shape.

Means and Medians

Several statistics that are routinely used to describe distributions assume that the distribution is normal. The two most prominent are the mean as a measure of center and the standard deviation as a measure of dispersion (the degree to which the values are spread out around the mean). We can easily get into trouble when we apply statistical measures that assume normality to abnormally shaped distributions. I've seen this problem often in academic research papers. They describe and compare skewed or otherwise abnormal distributions using means and standard deviations, at times leading to false conclusions.

Consider the two following distributions. Both have a mean of 10 years old and a standard deviation of 2.57 years, but they are skewed in opposite directions.

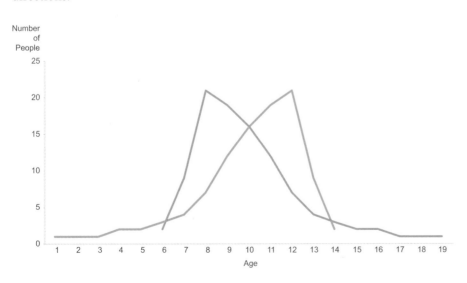

FIGURE 3.20

This graph exhibits three potential problems that we should keep in mind: 1) the mean is not a good measure of what's typical, 2) the standard deviation doesn't describe how the values are dispersed in either data set, and 3) the means and standard deviations suggest that these distributions are the same, which is clearly not the case. If one of these distributions describes the nature of variation in a set of experimental results from a control group versus a test group, and we conclude that they are the same based on equal means and standard deviations, our findings would be incorrect. We should use means and standard deviations only when describing normal distributions.

Let's look more closely at the distribution above that is skewed to the right (i.e., the green line, with its tail on the right and the peak on the left). Statisticians describe the direction in which a data set is skewed using the direction of the tail, not the location of the peak. This distribution appears by itself in the graph below.

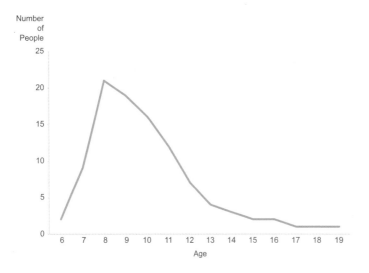

FIGURE 3.21

Looking at this distribution, can you see the problem caused by using standard deviation as a measure of dispersion around the mean?

Standard deviations below the mean, other than a standard deviation of -1, extend beyond the lowest value in this data set, illustrated below.

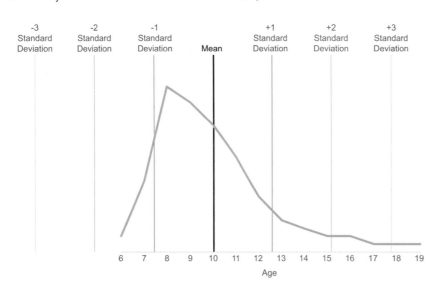

Figure 3.22

The problem with the standard deviation is that it uses the mean as its center, and the mean can only function as a reliable measure of center if the distribution is normal.

For some purposes, the characteristics of a normal distribution and the statistics that work exclusively for those characteristics are so handy that it's worthwhile to transform distributions of other shapes into normal distributions so that we can use those statistics. A few years ago I was helping a friend with some calculations that were needed to analyze the results of a neurological study. She was trying to compare distributions using means and standard deviations but was coming up with senseless results because the distributions were not normal. Instead, they were skewed to the left. I suggested that she shouldn't use means and standard deviations to describe and compare these data sets. She asked the head of her research department about this. Without pausing he said, "Just do a log transform." A bit sheepishly, her next question for me was, "What's a log transform?" The department head was instructing her to transform the values logarithmically, which would redistribute the values that were bunched up together in the upper peak in a way that would cause the distribution to take on a normal shape. Once the distribution was transformed in this manner, she could then use means and standard deviations to describe and compare the data sets.

Even though I understood the department head's intention, I found the nonchalance with which he instructed my friend to transform the data disconcerting. I kept thinking, "Don't we care about the actual shapes of these distributions?" and "Can't we leave the values as they are with skewed distributions and still compare them?" In fact, we can, but not as conveniently as by using means and standard deviations. Researchers with limited training in statistics are often unconcerned about the actual shapes of the distributions and the potential stories that reside in those shapes. They just want to compare distributions based on a simple statistic. I can't help but think that they're missing important observations when they handle data in this manner. Whether this is true or not, I'll leave to them, but when we're trying to preserve or improve the performance of an organization, we'll always begin by getting to know distributions for what they are.

When transformations, or what statistician John Tukey preferred to call *re-expressions*, are useful, several can be used to make distributions normal given different conditions. Expressing data in various ways for various purposes is standard fare for statisticians. According to Hartwig and Dearing:

> *Because reexpression is one of the primary means by which data can be explored for unanticipated patterns, the most useful approach is to treat scales of measurement as arbitrary. Data can then be reexpressed by any transformation so long as patterns that are discovered can be related back to the original data.*

Frederick Hartwig with Brian E. Dearing (1979). *Exploratory Data Analysis.* Sage Publications, page 12.

Logarithmic and square-root transformations are the most common, but there are many ways that values can be re-expressed to create a normal distribution. The methods used to re-express a distribution depend on its shape.

Suffice it to say that transformation can get complicated. Fortunately, in our work as data stewards, we will rarely need to transform values to get them to fit a normal distribution. Displaying data in a funnel plot, which we considered in the previous chapter, is one of those rare occasions. If you find yourself in a situation that you think would benefit from the addition of transformations to your analytical toolkit, I recommend that you read *Visualizing Data* by William Cleveland and *Exploratory Data Analysis* by Frederick Hartwig and Brian E. Dearing.

If the mean can't be used to describe the central tendency of a distribution that is skewed, what can? This is usually a job for a different measure of center: the *median*. When distributions are skewed, such as the example above, there are outliers in the data. Means are highly susceptible to influence by outliers.

Consider the following set of salaries:

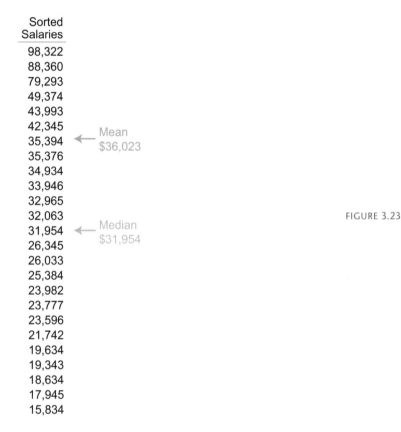

FIGURE 3.23

Which measure of central tendency does a better job of describing the typical salary in this data set: the mean or the median? The median does. The mean has been pulled toward the high end of this set of values by the top three salaries, which qualify as outliers. This distribution of salaries is skewed toward the high values. Here's the same set of values, this time visualized as a strip plot, which displays each value in a set as a data point along a single quantitative scale. In this strip plot, we can see how the mean has been pulled toward the higher end of the scale.

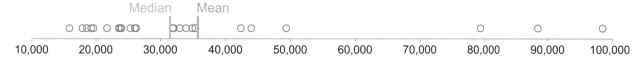

FIGURE 3.24

The mean is calculated by summing all of the values and dividing the total by the number of values in the set. Calculated in this manner, the mean is a measure of center that is heavily influenced by outliers. If we want to summarize the total financial impact on the bottom line of salary expenses per employee with a single measure of center, the mean works well. Think of the mean as a measure of a data set's quantitative center (i.e., the value below and above which 50% of the total amount resides).

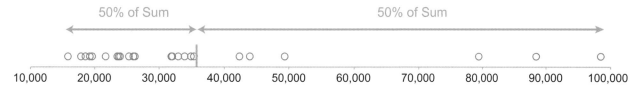

FIGURE 3.25

If, however, we want to express the salary that is typical of the set, the median is the better measure. The median is determined by sorting the entire set of values by size from high to low or vice versa and then selecting the value in the exact middle of the set. When a data set contains an even number of values, the median is determined by adding the two values in the middle together and dividing by two. Calculated in this way, the median is resistant to the influence of outliers. Think of the median as a measure of a data set's ordinal center (i.e., the value below and above which 50% of the values reside).

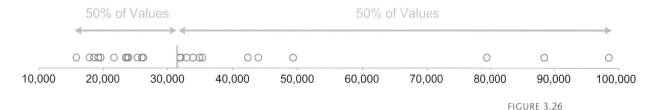

FIGURE 3.26

Graphs for Exploring a Single Distribution

To explore a single distribution, we'll begin with an overview of variation within each measure, but we don't want a view that summarizes the distribution to such a high level that significant details are hidden. By beginning with a detailed view of the distribution, we'll discover characteristics that will help us determine an appropriate highly summarized view for later. We want to begin with a view that allows us to see individual values along with a sense of the distribution's overall shape. For this, we use a graph that might be unfamiliar to you: a *quantile plot*.

Quantile Plots

A quantile plot is quite simple. It arranges a set of values in ranked order from lowest to highest, represents each value as a dot, and groups the values into sets of 25% each. The boundaries of these sets are marked by the following three values: quartile 1 (25th percentile), median (a.k.a., 50th percentile or quartile 2), and quartile 3 (75th percentile). Here's a quantile plot of 25 men's heights:

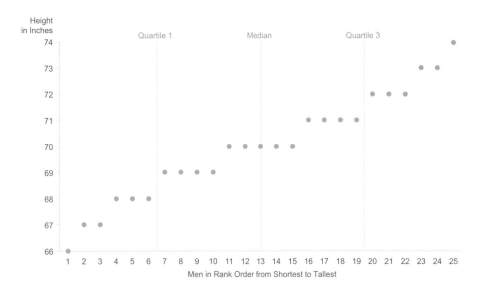

FIGURE 3.27

Here we can see each value in the set, in addition to summary information in the form of the spread from the lowest to highest values and the central tendency in the form of the median. The addition of quartiles 1 and 3 gives us a sense of the distribution's shape, with the middle 50% of men tightly packed around the median height of 70 inches (5'10"), from 69 to 71 inches, and both the lowest and highest 25% of men both spread across three-inch ranges from 66 to 68 inches (the shortest) and 72 to 74 inches (the tallest). Imagine that these men were selected at random on the street during rush hour in the financial district of San Francisco. We would expect the distribution to be fairly normal in shape, but in this case I've fabricated a perfectly normal distribution. Here's the same set of values displayed in a way that's more familiar:

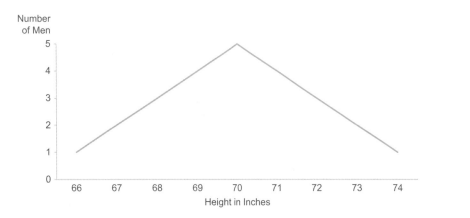

FIGURE 3.28

Indeed, we have a perfectly normal distribution. Notice that the familiar bell-shaped curve of a normal distribution has a different shape when displayed in a quantile plot. The shape is linear, rising upwards from left to right, illustrated by the line in the quantile plot below.

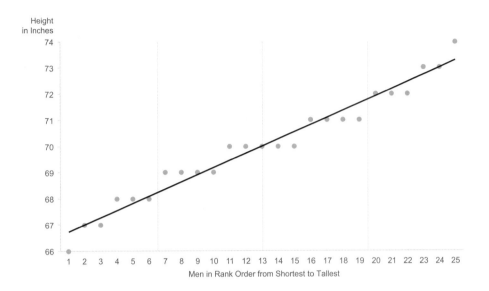

FIGURE 3.29

Let's look at another set of values that better illustrates the advantages of starting a distribution review with a quantile plot. Below we see a new set of values represented first in the familiar way using a line, and, below that, in a quantile plot.

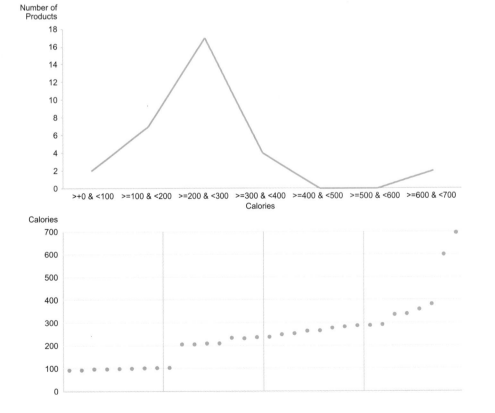

FIGURE 3.30

Compare the two graphs to see whether you can identify any information that can be found in the quantile plot that isn't visible in the upper line graph.

Did you find two primary differences? First, we can see, at the low end of the calorie scale, that all of the values between 0 and 200 are near 100 and that there is a big gap between values close to 100 and the next highest, which are greater than 200. On the right, we can see that the two highest values differ by 100 calories. These characteristics are significant, but they are entirely hidden in the upper graph because it counts the number of values in intervals (bins of a particular range) along the X axis rather than showing individual values.

One of the greatest strengths of quantile plots is the way that they enable comparisons of distributions, but we'll get to that later.

Histograms

The graph most often used for summarizing distributions is the *histogram*. It divides a spread of values into several intervals of equal size and uses bars to display the number or percentage of values contained in each interval. Here's a simple example of people by age groups (intervals) of 10 years each:

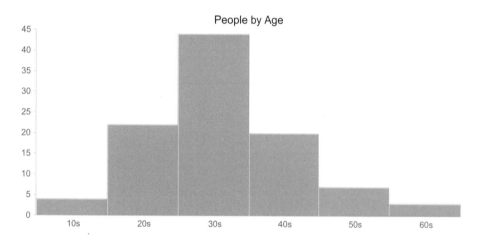

FIGURE 3.31

Histograms are popular because they are a simple way to get a high-level overview of a distribution's shape and to compare the number or percentage of values between one interval and the next simply by comparing the heights of the bars. Both the histogram and the graph that we'll look at next, the *frequency polygon*, remove the details (i.e., the individual values) by aggregating values into intervals and then counting the number or calculating the percentage in each. If we've already seen the details in a quantile plot, there's little chance that we'll be misled by the loss of detail when we now focus primarily on the distribution's overall shape in a histogram. Here are a histogram and a quantile plot shown together, which illustrates the ways that they differ yet complement one another.

Conventionally, the bars in histograms have no gaps between them. Although this isn't necessary, it's probably best to remove gaps when we show distributions to others, especially if there are any statisticians in the group, to avoid an argument.

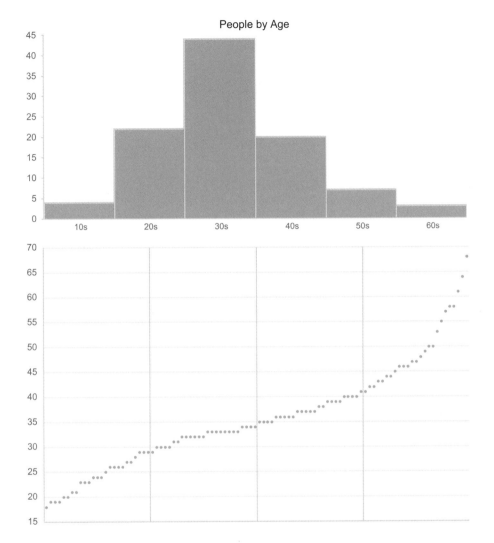

FIGURE 3.32

Features that aren't revealed in a histogram are the central tendency and the precise lowest and highest values because the intervals often extend somewhat below the lowest value and somewhat above the highest. For example, the histogram above shows us that there are four teenagers in the group, but we don't know their exact ages; the histogram doesn't help us if we want to know the age of the youngest, for example. However, if we examine the data in a quantile plot first, we can see that the youngest teenager is 18 before switching to the more highly summarized view in the histogram.

We must decide the size of the intervals to use when constructing a histogram or frequency polygon, which is the next graph that we'll cover. The size of intervals determines the number of intervals. In the histogram above of people by age, I chose 10-year intervals, but why not intervals of 5, 12, or 15 years each? When dealing with people's ages, 10-year intervals are easy to understand; that's part of the reason that I chose them. But if the spread had extended only from 30 through 59 years, using 10-year intervals would have given me only three bins, which would be too broad to provide a good summary of the distribution's shape. What we strive for is an interval size that is not so large that we lose sight of meaningful variation within the bins but not so small that the distribution's shape is overly jagged, with too much detail to get a sense of the overall shape. Somewhere between these extremes lie effectively sized intervals. No strict rule or formula will determine those intervals for us. We will occasionally need to experiment, trying intervals of different sizes to find the one that works. Some software products help us do this by providing a simple control, such as a slider, that allows us to dynamically change the size of the intervals and watch the histogram change during the process. When we spot the size that provides the best view, we stop moving the slider, and we're done. (It's nice when software designers provide a feature in a product that makes it easy to interact with the data in frequently useful ways.)

Frequency Polygons

The frequency polygon is like a histogram except that it uses a line rather than bars to represent the values. Here's the same distribution as above, displayed as a frequency polygon.

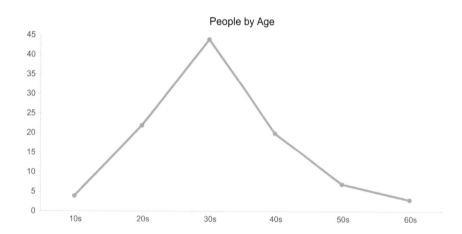

FIGURE 3.33

Frequency polygons have two potential advantages over histograms:

- They show the shape of the distribution more clearly.
- They make it possible to compare the shapes of several distributions in a single graph.

We'll see the second advantage in practice later when we look at ways to compare distributions. For now, while examining one distribution at a time, we'll use frequency polygons when we want to focus primarily on the distribution's shape.

A useful enhancement to a standard frequency polygon is the use of background fill colors to divide the values into sets of 25% each. In the following example, the darkest shade of gray in the background marks the midspread, the gray line marks the median, and the lighter shade of gray marks the ranges across which the lowest and highest 25% of the values fall.

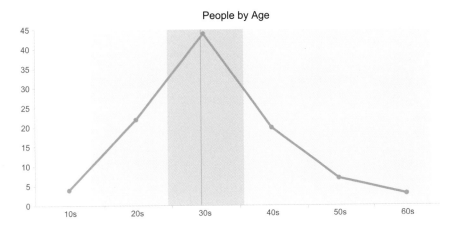

FIGURE 3.34

This background coloration enriches the information that is communicated without overcomplicating the graph. I haven't seen any software that does this as a standard feature, but some products provide the means to do this with little effort.

Strip Plots

Besides the quantile plot, another graph that displays individual values in a distribution is the *strip plot*. The strip plot consists of a single quantitative scale and an individual data point, such as a dot, for each value in the set.

FIGURE 3.35

A strip plot is like a quantile plot except that the quantile plot eliminates the problem of over-plotting (data points on top of data points) by distributing the data points horizontally from lowest to highest value. In the figure below, the quantile plot on the left and strip plot on the right display the same set of values.

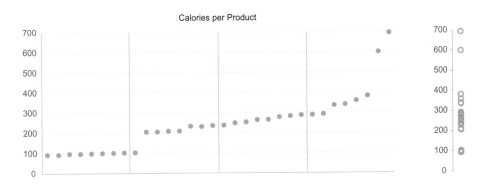

FIGURE 3.36

Lines could be added to a strip plot to mark the quartiles, which would make it similar to the quantile plot in function.

Just as the overviews of distributions in histograms and frequency polygons are complemented by quantile plots with their display of the individual values, they may also be complemented by strip plots, as shown below.

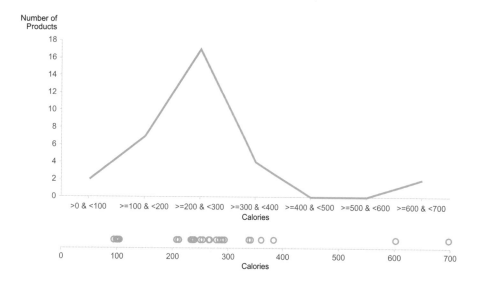

FIGURE 3.37

Graphs for Comparing Multiple Distributions

The distribution comparisons that we'll make here will involve categories. As I mentioned previously, categories provide the basic framework on which most of our observations about a data set will hang. We're interested in finding out how distributions of values within measures differ among items in a category. For example, how does the distribution of order amounts differ among products, or how do the ages of patients who were treated for the flu differ among hospitals? And, often most importantly, how do distributions change through time?

Before moving on to the graphs that we'll use, let me share a trick that often simplifies comparisons. Imagine that you want to compare the ages of patients who are treated for the flu among a set of hospitals, clinics, and doctor's offices that vary significantly in size. Hospitals see thousands of patients per month, but a doctor's office might only see 200 patients during the same period. This difference in scale will make distribution comparisons difficult if our quantitative scale is based on the number of patients treated. In the following example, the shapes of the distributions for the two doctors' offices (the bottom two lines) are impossible to see.

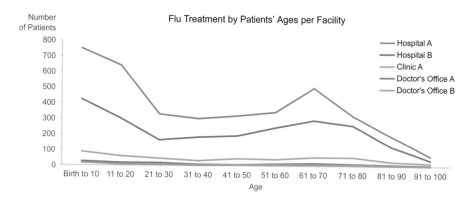

FIGURE 3.38

The solution is simple: switch the scale from counts to the percentage break-
down of patients by age group for each facility. In the example below, the
quantitative scale indicates the percentage of a particular facility's patients who
were treated for the flu by age group. If we add together all the values for any of
the lines, they equal 100%.

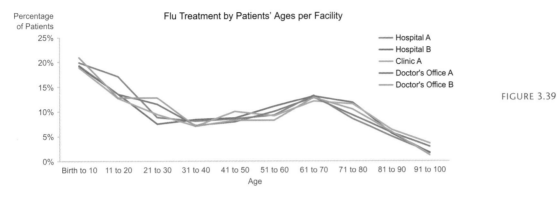

FIGURE 3.39

Now, no matter how much the data sets differ in size, we can easily compare
their distributions.

Box Plots

The *box plot* was one of John Tukey's wonderful inventions for visualizing
statistical data. It will be our general-purpose graph for comparing distributions
because it's easy to use and can handle many distributions at a time. The
example below can be used to compare the lengths of phone calls related to
various products that are received by a technical support department.

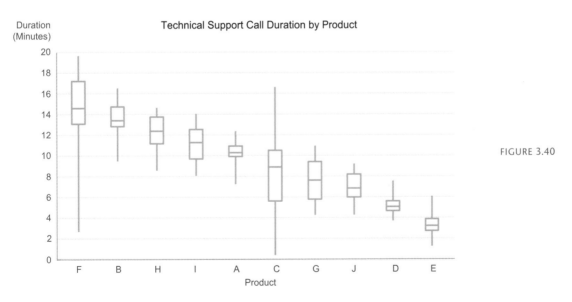

FIGURE 3.40

Although the parts of a box plot can represent various measures of distribution, the following are typical:

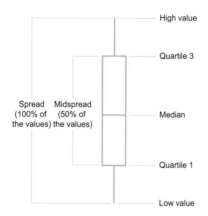

FIGURE 3.41

The full name of a box plot, as originally coined by Tukey, is a *box-and-whisker plot*. The lines that encode the top and bottom ranges of values are called whiskers, and the rectangle in the middle, which encodes the midspread, is called the box. This example displays a five-value distribution summary, consisting of the lowest value, quartile 1, the median, quartile 3, and the highest value. In other words, the values are divided into four sets of 25% each. Given how much they can tell us about distributions, box plots are quite elegant in their simplicity.

Box plots usually go further by displaying outliers independently from the whiskers. This adds a bit of complexity, but it's worth it. Here's the technical support call example that we looked at above, this time with the outliers represented as individual dots.

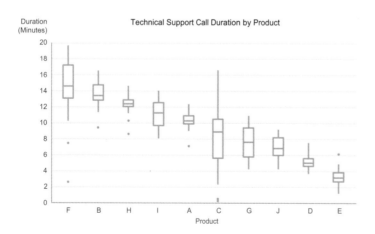

FIGURE 3.42

When outliers are displayed independently, the whiskers only extend to the highest or lowest values in the distribution, excluding the outliers. In the example above, we can see that all of the phone calls related to product F that fall within the shortest 25% of call lengths were longer than 10.1 minutes except for one call that lasted only 7.5 minutes and another that lasted a mere 2.7 minutes. It's useful to see outliers as separate from routine values. When the center mark represents the median, and the box marks the midspread, outliers are defined as all values that fall beyond a distance equal to 1.5 times the midspread either above or below the midspread, illustrated below.

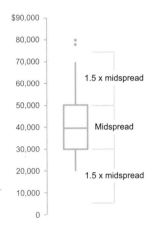

FIGURE 3.43

The simplicity of the box plot is based in part on the fact that it reduces a distribution to five values, plus outliers. However, this summary can lack details that we sometimes need to see. When more details are needed, the next graphs that we'll consider—multiple quantile plots and q-q plots—are handy.

Multiple Quantile Plots

Multiple quantile plots can be used to compare multiple distributions in detail. This is simple to do when the data sets that we want to compare contain the same number of values, but it's difficult when this isn't the case, as in the example below.

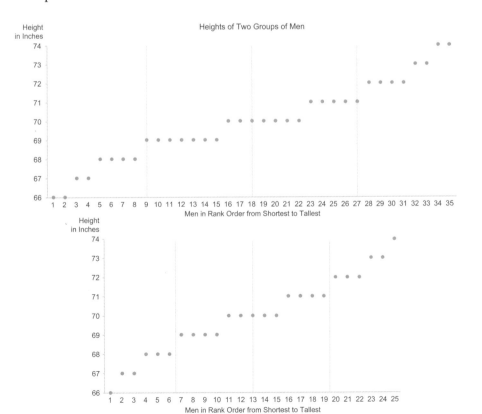

FIGURE 3.44

When the number of values varies among data sets that we want to compare, we can use a technique to make quantile plots more comparable. The technique creates consistency in the display of the data sets by positioning values uniformly along a shared scale on the X axis. This technique has been applied to the two quantile plots below.

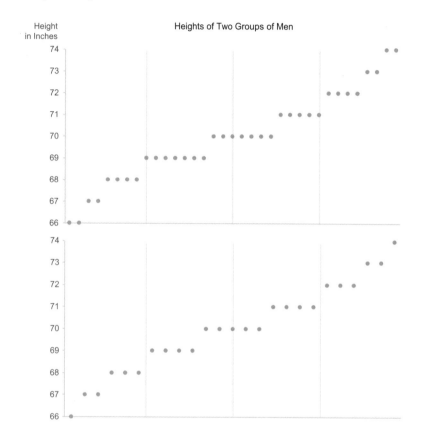

FIGURE 3.45

Even though the upper data set contains 25 values, and the lower one contains 35 values, the values in each quantile plot have been uniformly positioned along a shared scale.

The same two distributions appear in the box plot below, but in the box plot we can no longer compare individual values and see the subtle way in which these two distributions differ, such as the slight skew in the set of 35 values that doesn't appear in the smaller set.

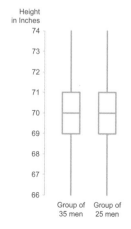

FIGURE 3.46

The traditional method of constructing quantile plots standardizes their X axes to one common scale extending from 0 to 1. This involves some simple math. The position of each value can be determined by the following formula:

X axis position = (the ranked position of the value from lowest to highest - 0.5) ÷ the total number of values

For example, consider the following set of seven values:

5   1   9   3   14   9   7

In sequential order from lowest to highest, these values appear as:

1   3   5   7   9   9   14

The position of the first two values along the X axis are therefore:

(1 - 0.5) ÷ 7 = 0.071
(2 - 0.5) ÷ 7 = 0.214

and the position of the final value is:

(7 - 0.5) ÷ 7 = 0.929

Only the number of values and their order are needed to determine their positions. This formula can be used to spread a set of values uniformly along the X axis no matter how many values there are.

Q-Q Plots

Even more useful for comparing two distributions to see how they differ, especially with large data sets, is the *q-q plot* (quantile-quantile plot), which is a special version of a scatter plot that was invented by Martin Wilk and Ram Gnanadesikan. Here's an example that compares the scores that were earned on a test by 457 male and 502 female high school students:

Another way to get two quantile plots to have equal-width plot areas so they can be easily compared is to adjust their widths manually. For example, in Excel it would be easy to create two graphs in the usual way and to then resize one's width to match the other's. Or, better yet, we can create a chart for one data set in Excel, make a copy of it, and select the other data set in the second chart, which will produce two charts of equal size.

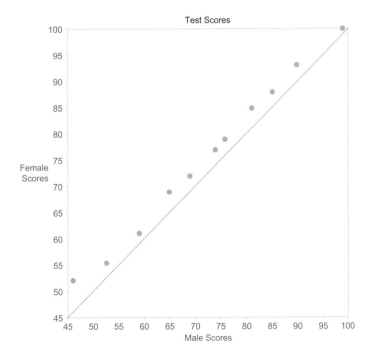

FIGURE 3.47

The data points in the graph don't represent individual student scores. Instead, they represent a series of percentiles associated with each set of scores. In this example, I've summarized each set of values using the following percentiles: 1st (lowest value), 10th, 20th, 30th, 40th, 50th, 60th, 70th, 80th, 90th, and 100th (highest value). Here's a strip plot that displays these percentiles for male test scores:

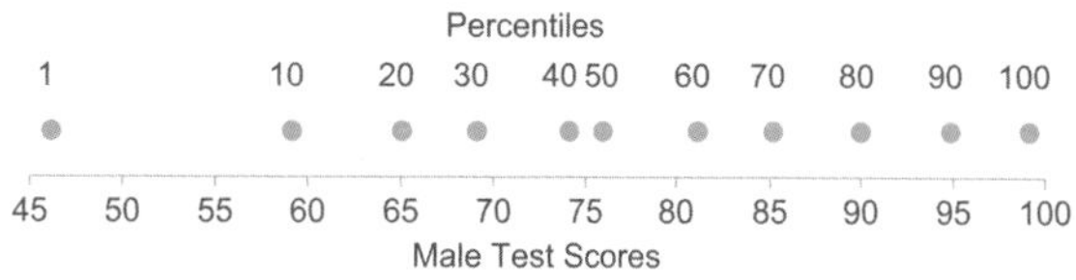

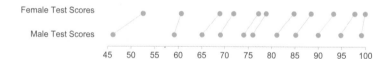

FIGURE 3.48

And here are the same percentiles for female test scores:

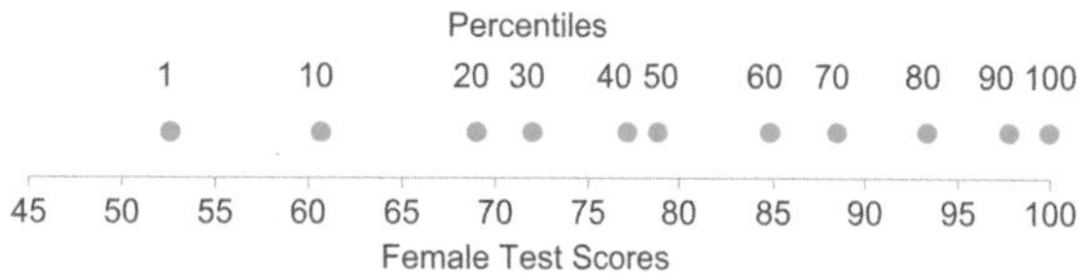

FIGURE 3.49

We could combine both sets of percentiles in a single strip plot to compare them, as I've done below.

FIGURE 3.50

I've drawn lines to connect each pair of percentiles to show that in every case the female score is higher than the male score to varying degrees. Now that it's clear that we're examining paired sets of percentiles that summarize male and female test scores, let's look again at the q-q plot of this same data set, this time with each pair of percentiles labeled.

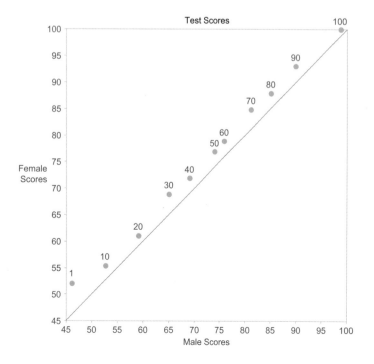

FIGURE 3.51

The diagonal line in the plot area is not a fit model. Rather, it connects the lower left and upper right corners to divide the plot area into equal halves. It does this to make it easy to see how the two data sets differ for each pair of percentiles. For this to work properly, the quantitative scales on the X and Y axes must be identical, in this case ranging from scores of 45 to 100. Whenever a data point is on the diagonal line, the two data sets have the same value for that percentile. Whenever a data point appears above or below the diagonal line, the two distributions differ at that particular percentile. When a data point is located above the line, the value for that percentile is higher for the variable on the Y axis, and when it falls below the line, it is higher for the variable on the X axis. In this q-q plot, we can easily see by the fact that all of the dots appear above the diagonal line that females scored better than males across the entire distribution.

In the next example, we can compare the scores of the same group of students for a different test. In this case I've included the following percentiles: 1, 2, 3, 4, 5, 10, 20, 30, 40, 50, 60, 70, 80, 90, 96, 97, 98, 99, and 100. By including additional percentiles at the high and low ends of the scale, we can potentially see subtler differences among the highest and lowest test scores where potential outliers might be found.

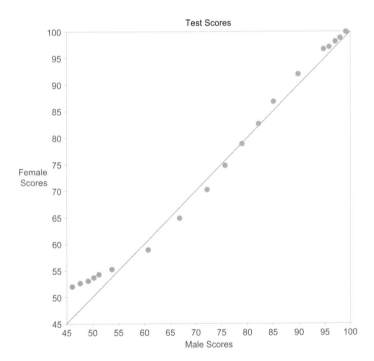

FIGURE 3.52

For this test, the comparison of male and female scores is different from the previous example. Here we see that females scored better than males in the low and high ends of the distributions, but did worse than males in the middle range, scoring lower than males at percentiles 20, 30, 40, and 50, and matching males at percentile 60. I hope that it is now clear how q-q plots work and that they can be especially useful when we need to compare distributions that consist of many values. We can use q-q plots for comparing distributions of relatively small data sets, but using percentiles in this manner to compare distributions works best with data sets that include at least 100 values each.

Before moving on, it's worthwhile to think a bit more about percentiles because they're defined a little differently for various uses. The definition that I've been using in this book is that a percentile is the value in a data set at or below which a specified percentage of values fall. For example, the 25th percentile (a.k.a., 1st quartile) is the value in a data set at or below which 25% of the values in the data set fall. When defined in this manner, the lowest possible percentile is 1 and the highest is 100.

Sometimes, however, a percentile is defined as the value *below which* (not *at or below which*) a specified percentage of values fall. This is how the term is usually defined when schools report how particular students are doing compared to their peers. In this case, a student who is performing at the 75th percentile is doing better than 75% of his peers, not equal to or better than 75% of his peers. When defined in this manner, a percentile of 100 is not possible because a particular student's performance score could not be higher than 100% of the scores because his score is part of the set and therefore it cannot be higher than itself. Also, when defined in this manner, the lowest possible percentile is 0, for the student with the lowest score would not have any scores that fall below his.

When comparing distributions, it really doesn't matter which of these definitions that we use, just as long as we define percentiles in a consistent manner and explain how we're defining the term when we present information to others.

There is one more way in which percentiles are handled differently for various purposes and by different software products. The textbook definition of a percentile that is typically taught in a statistics course is that a percentile is always an actual value that exists in the data set. For example, in a data set with 457 values, such as the set of male test scores, to determine the value of percentile 10, we would multiply 457 by 0.1 (i.e., 10%), resulting in 45.7, then we would round the value up to the next whole number, which is 46, and finally, counting the values in order from the lowest to the highest we would find the 46th value in the data set, which would be our value for the 10th percentile. In the set of male test scores that we were examining previously, which ranged from scores of 46 through 99, the 10th percentile was a score of 54. This is called the *nearest rank* method of determining a percentile. Using this method, a small data set consisting of only 10 values—15, 19, 27, 33, 34, 39, 41, 44, 49, and 51—percentiles 1 through 10 would all have the same value of 15, the lowest value in the set.

As an alternative to the textbook definition, many software products don't necessarily find an actual value in the data set but instead calculate values that are unique for each percentile. Excel's *PERCENTILE* function works in this way. Using Excel, the lowest percentile for the 10 values listed above would still be 15, but the 10th percentile would be 18.6. I prefer the textbook nearest rank method, but for our purposes when comparing distributions of large data sets, either approach will work fine.

Excel's PERCENTILE function is a bit strange in that it allows percentiles to range from 0 to 100, which doesn't fit either of the standard definitions of a percentile representing (1) a specified percentage of values at or below a particular value or (2) a specified percentage below a particular value. Using Excel's PERCENTILE function to calculate percentile 0 in the list of 10 values 15, 19, 27, 33, 34, 39, 41, 44, 49, and 51 would produce the result of 15, the lowest value in the list. Using it to calculate percentile 1, however, would produce the value 15.36, and using it to calculate percentile 100 would produce 51, the highest value.

Distribution Deviation Graphs

When we want to focus even more closely on differences between distributions, the *distribution deviation graph* is a useful improvement over the q-q plot. Below, the same male-versus-female test scores that appear in the q-q plot above are displayed with positive values for higher female scores and negative values for higher male scores. The values were simply calculated as female minus male scores for each of the percentiles.

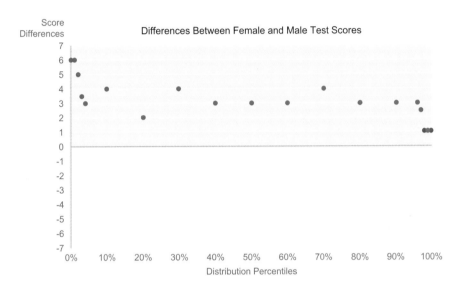

FIGURE 3.53

The pink and blue colors aren't necessary, of course, but in this case they are a simple way to distinguish greater female (pink) versus male (blue) test scores. It isn't necessary to extend the quantitative scale along the Y axis below zero as I did above because in this case there are no negative values. However, including the negative range emphasizes the absence of superior male test scores. The superior performance of females can be seen even more clearly in this distribution deviation graph than in the q-q plot.

Here's another example, this time with a mixture of positive and negative values.

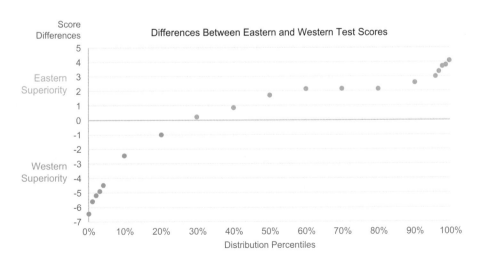

FIGURE 3.54

In this case, for some reason students in the western region outperform students in the eastern region in the low percentiles, but starting at the 30th percentile and continuing above that point, students in the eastern region do better. I prefer distribution deviation graphs over q-q plots because I find it easier to compare vertical differences relative to a horizontal baseline of zero. See whether this is true for you as well. If it is, use distribution deviation graphs to do with greater ease what statisticians typically do with q-q plots.

Frequency Polygons

Nothing does a better job of displaying a two-dimensional shape than a line reduced to a simple contour. For this reason, frequency polygons are often the best form of display for a simple summary of a distribution's shape. The same is true when we wish to compare the shapes of distributions, assuming that we're only comparing a few. Ordinarily, up to five or six lines can be displayed in a frequency polygon without undue clutter. In the frequency polygon below, which we looked at previously, each line represents a healthcare facility's distribution of patients by age who were treated for the flu, and the box plot below it shows the same data.

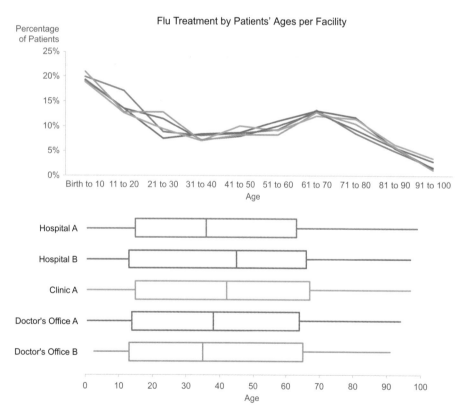

FIGURE 3.55

The frequency polygon and the box plot have different strengths that lend them to different uses. The frequency polygon does not show precise ages, such as the lowest age in each group (because age counts are aggregated into intervals of 10 years each), nor does it show a measure of center or midspread as a box plot does. But in a frequency polygon, we can see subtle differences in the shapes of the distribution. For example, notice that Hospital A has a significantly higher percentage of patients in the 11 to 20 age group. Also, notice that the 21 to 30 age group exhibits the greatest degree of variation among the four facilities, and the 61 to 70 age group exhibits the least degree of variation. For comparative details such as these, the frequency polygon excels.

Exploratory Signals

Imagine that we work for a real estate company, and we're examining variation in the prices of homes that the company has sold. Overall, we've noticed that the distribution of prices is bimodal with a peak among low-priced homes and another among high-priced homes, and far fewer sales in the middle price range.

FIGURE 3.56

Unless it is the company's objective to focus on the low and high ends of the housing market with less concern for houses in the middle, this would stand out as a potential signal. We seem to be neglecting the middle market, but why? We need to determine whether lower sales in the middle market are a sign of something that we're doing (or in this case, failing to do), rather than simply a smaller inventory of houses in the middle range. To figure this out, we can add some context to the picture. Showing the overall distribution of sales by all real estate companies compared to our company's distribution of sales provides the comparison that we need.

FIGURE 3.57

We now know that the overall market isn't causing this pattern. To investigate further, we might ask, "Is this pattern the same for all geographical regions?" A frequency polygon with one line per region, assuming that we only have a few regions, gives us this answer.

FIGURE 3.58

Perhaps this pattern varies per real estate agent. A box plot with one box per agent would reveal this.

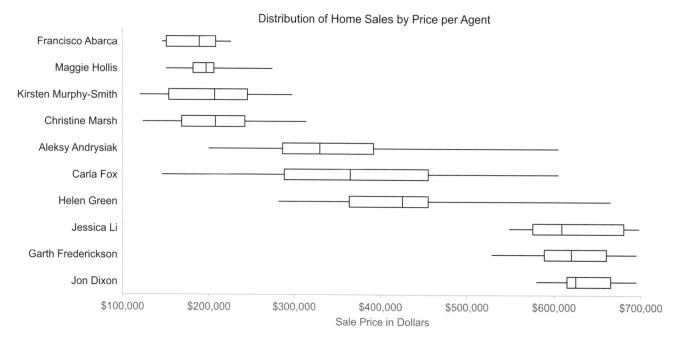

FIGURE 3.59

Given our knowledge of the domain, we notice that the seven agents who are exclusively selling high-priced houses are the same ones who were invited to participate in the "Golden Key" luxury home program that rewards them with special commissions. Perhaps something similar is going on for the agents that are focusing on low-priced homes. This time, let's display the distributions for each of the special programs that pay commissions.

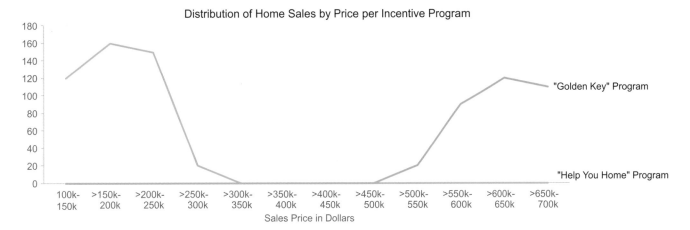

FIGURE 3.60

We now know the cause behind this signal. Before we do something to disrupt the bimodal pattern of sales, however, we'll want to think long and hard about the benefits of the various options available to us. It would be best to boost sales in the middle range without reducing sales on the low and high ends. Perhaps another incentive program to balance things out is in order, or perhaps, given the fact that our sales agents are all busy, it would be better to hire more agents to make sure that increased sales in the middle aren't achieved by robbing sales from elsewhere.

The signals that emerge during our initial exploration give us an opportunity for intentional action. With this knowledge we can attempt to sculpt the patterns of variation within measures to match our objectives. We can make decisions, initiate actions, and then monitor the results. Once the patterns stabilize in a way that matches our objectives, our main task in signal detection will shift to tracking changes in the desired pattern that reveal changes in the underlying process. In other words, most future signals in variation within measures will reveal themselves as changes through time. We'll learn ways to spot these signals graphically in *Chapter 9 – Install Signal Sensors*.

"Space, the final frontier." No, we are not taking a voyage on the Starship Enterprise, and space is not actually our final frontier as stewards. Only a few of us, such as those who work with astronomical data, will be concerned with outer space. Most of us will remain earthbound, in the realm of geographical space, and some of us will narrow our focus to even smaller realms, such as locations within buildings.

Of the four dimensions that we perceive and navigate throughout our lives—height, width, depth, and time—all but one are spatial. Much of our perceptual and cognitive ability helps us locate and track ourselves and other objects in space. Spatial locations are examples of categorical data, and we've already examined variation within categories in general. However, because space is one of the fundamental categories in human experience, it deserves special attention.

Spatial Relationships

As stewards, we're primarily concerned with the location of quantitative values in space rather than the nature of space itself, such as the shapes and sizes of geographical regions. How do these values relate to one another spatially? We're interested in where things are, where things happen, and to what degree. "Where?" is an essential question not just in life but in data sensemaking as well. "In which region is the flu epidemic most severe?" "Where do our customers live and in what numbers?" "Where are our services most lacking yet needed?" Space is the context or backdrop for values when the locations of those values are significant.

FIGURE 4.1

Visualizations for Spatial Sensemaking

Many, perhaps most, of our spatial interests can be explored and examined using the same techniques that we used for examining other categories in *Chapter 2 – Variation within Categories*. For instance, we might use a bar graph to determine how each U.S. state contributes to the whole of our sales. At times we'll need visualizations that position values in space, such as on a map or the floor plan of a building, but this will be necessary less often than you might imagine. What if we wanted to answer the question, "What is the relative impact of HIV-AIDS, by county, in the state of California?" Viewing counts of known infections per 1,000 people per county on a map wouldn't answer this question. Imagine trying to put the counties in order by comparing the sizes of bubbles or the intensities of fill colors on a map? Not an easy task, but a simple bar graph with the counties sorted by the number of infections per 1,000 people would support the task well.

Viewing data in spatial representations is only useful when we need to understand one of the following:

1. The locations of values relative to one another
2. The locations of values relative to the locations of other phenomena
3. The pattern or amount of space across which values are distributed

A map would be useful to answer the question, "Do particular counties in California have fewer rates of influenza than we would expect, relative to nearby counties?" Imagine a map of California on which each county is filled with a particular color that varies in intensity from light for low rates of influenza to dark for high. We would be able to easily spot a county filled with a light color that's surrounded by counties filled with dark colors. We can answer this particular question only by seeing the locations of values relative to one another.

When Dr. John Snow placed bars on a map of London to show the locations and numbers of people who had died of cholera during an epidemic in the 1850s and then marked the locations of the wells from which people drew their drinking water, he needed to see the relative locations of those two variables to demonstrate his hypothesis that cholera was being transmitted through the water supply.

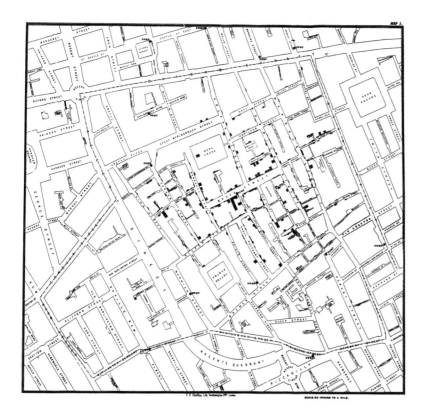

FIGURE 4.2

Similarly, if we needed to track the geographical spread of influenza from day to day, we would need to compare daily snapshots of the cases on a map to see the extent to which they're dispersed and the pattern of dispersion. Only a map-based display would give us this view.

Now that many software products make it possible to view data on a map, maps are often mistakenly used to answer questions or tell stories that are better handled in other ways. Just because we can place data on a map doesn't mean we should. It's useful to distinguish effective uses of a map from ineffective uses. Take a minute to consider each of the following questions to determine which should be answered using a map versus another form of display:

1. How many of the library system's current patrons come from low-income neighborhoods, and where should we locate a new branch to best serve them?
2. In which states are our highest sales and profits?
3. Our organization has computer servers in several different cities around the world. There has been a spike in online attacks against the organization recently. Are these attacks originating from any regions in particular?
4. The Transit Authority needs to eliminate two bus routes to reduce costs. Which two bus routes could be eliminated while causing the least disruption for riders?
5. How long does it take shipments to reach our customers, and are there areas where the delivery times are unexpectedly poor?
6. Which countries participated in the last Olympics, and how many athletes did each country send?
7. Based on incidents of crime, which neighborhoods or intersections would benefit most from an increased police presence?
8. We work for a boutique furniture store that focuses on affluent customers. Of the affluent neighborhoods near our store, are there any that contribute a significantly higher or lower concentration of customers than we would expect?
9. How do our profits in the various European countries compare to profits in the various Asian countries?
10. What is the temperature of each room in our large, multi-story office complex, and are there rooms that are too hot or cold?

My answers to these questions are on page 104 in the margin. It's possible that you'll think of circumstances in which my answers wouldn't apply, and that's fine. What's important is that you spend time thinking about the best way to make sense of the data, and that doesn't always follow a rigid set of rules.

Encoding Values in Space

Quantitative values are typically encoded on maps using one of two methods:

- Objects such as bubbles that vary in size (and sometimes also in color intensity)
- Color-filled regions that vary in intensity

Neither method is ideal because both rely on visual attributes that our brains are not designed to easily and accurately decode and compare. We use these methods only because the visual attributes that work best for our brains—in particular, 2-D positions and lengths of objects with a common baseline—cannot be used on a map. Position can't be used for encoding quantitative values because, on a map, position must be used to represent locations. Bars that vary in length cannot share a common baseline because they must be positioned at particular locations on the map that are not aligned. Consequently, when using a map, we encode quantitative values using variation in size and color intensity because these are usually the best options available.

These encoding methods have been used by cartographers for generations, and many fine books teach best practices for their use and design. I won't try to duplicate the information that can be found in these resources, but I will introduce a few basic guidelines.

Bubbles are nothing but circles that vary in size. When it's useful to encode two quantitative variables using a single bubble, the bubble can vary in color intensity as well. Bubbles can represent aggregate values associated with entire regions or individual values at particular locations. In the following example, bubbles are used to encode the sum of sales revenues per state.

In 2013, I introduced a means of displaying values on a map, called *bricks*, as a perceptually superior alternative to bubbles, but bricks are not quite as versatile as bubbles and are not yet supported by commercial software products. Perhaps in time bricks will become an available option.

FIGURE 4.3

In the next example, bubbles are used to encode the sales to individual customers in the state of Florida. This example uses only the outlines of the bubbles so that overlapping bubbles don't hide (occlude) one another.

FIGURE 4.4

Whenever variation in color intensity is used to represent a range of quantitative values on a map (e.g., a weather map that uses colors to display variation in air temperature) or in any other form of display, the resulting graphic is called a *heat map*. A map that fills entire geographical regions with heat-map colors is called a *choropleth map*, such as the example below.

FIGURE 4.5

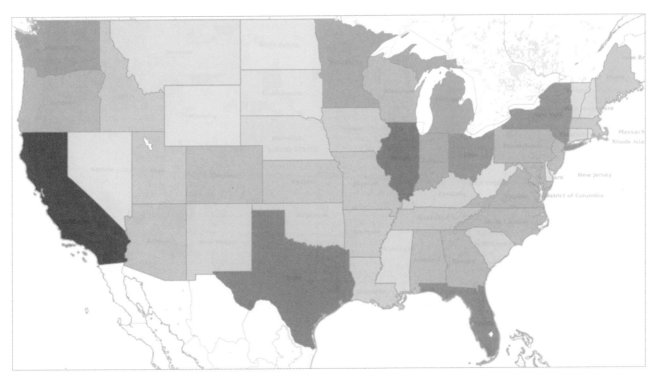

Unlike maps with bubbles, choropleth maps cannot be used to pinpoint the locations of individual values, only to display aggregate values for entire regions. In this sense, bubbles are more versatile than color-filled regions, and they sometimes have other advantages as well. Consider the following map of the lower portion of Africa:

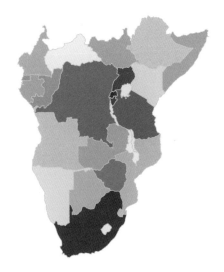

FIGURE 4.6

Knowing that values range from the lowest, represented by light shades of gray, to the highest, represented by dark shades, which country would you say has the highest value? Don't worry about the country's name; just note its location. Did you pick the country at the bottom (South Africa)? Most people would, and they'd be wrong. The country with the highest value is Rwanda, identified by the white arrow on the map below:

FIGURE 4.7

South Africa is 84% gray and Rwanda is 86% gray. South Africa may seem darker, however, for two reasons: first, because it is larger, and the larger an object is, the easier its color is to see; second, because it is surrounded by lighter-colored regions, which makes it appear darker in contrast.

Which country has the lowest value? Actually, the three marked by arrows on the next map are all precisely 10% gray, but differences in the color intensities surrounding them makes this fact difficult to discern.

FIGURE 4.8

From these examples, we can see how our perception of an object's color is strongly influenced by the colors surrounding the object. Our ability to discern information from choropleth maps is hampered by this perceptual problem. Bubbles are not entirely immune to this kind of misperception, but they are less susceptible. For this reason, I usually rely on bubbles to encode the values that are of most interest and reserve the color-fill method for secondary, contextual information.

The following example shows three separate quantitative variables: revenues per state (bubble size), profits per state (bubble color intensity), and per-capita income per state (regional color fills).

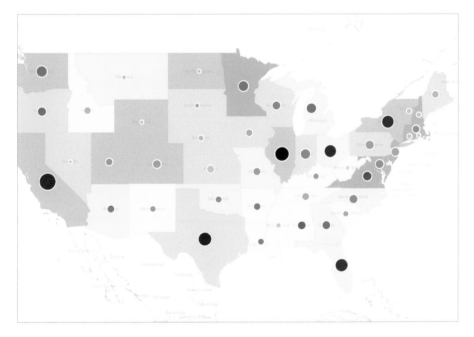

FIGURE 4.9

Notice the light-gray outlines around the bubbles. These are known as "halos." They help separate the bubbles from the background surrounding them, which reduces the influence of the colored backgrounds on our perception of the bubbles' colors.

I used regional color fills to encode per-capita income on this map because this income information provides context, so clarity of perception is less important for this variable than for the variable of primary interest, revenues. Profits are the secondary variable of interest. Median per-capita (household) income is there to help us understand whether regional income differences might explain why revenues are greater in some areas than others.

Notice how the map itself sits politely in the background, allowing the values to stand out clearly. Geographical space is the backdrop on which the data is being displayed, so the map itself should be subdued, not featured. It is there so that we can identify the locations of the values, not to give us a lesson in geography. For visualizations such as this one, it works best to use maps that are specifically designed for featuring values and therefore minimize the amount of geographical detail they show, rather than using maps designed for other purposes that require more geographical detail. Placing values on a map that was designed for displaying driving directions, such as a Google map, includes distracting geographical information that's of no use to us here.

When color is used to encode a range of values, the color should vary in intensity from light to dark. If I gave the five different colors shown below to one of my classes and asked the students to put the colors in order, every possible sequence would result. Why?

FIGURE 4.10

Because these colors vary only in hue, not in intensity, so there is no perceptual cue to indicate a sequence for them.

However, if I gave the same group of students the following five colors, everyone would produce the sequence shown or its opposite.

FIGURE 4.11

When colors vary in intensity from light to dark or from pale to fully saturated (or a combination of both), they have an obvious sequence. They may vary slightly in hue, as the series of colors above varies slightly from yellow through orange to red, but the primary difference among them is their values of lightness and/or saturation.

The series of colors above serves as a sequential scale; it runs in one direction only. The series below serves as a diverging scale; it runs in two directions around a breakpoint in the middle.

If you're using software that doesn't provide well-designed sequences of colors, take advantage of the suggestions that you'll find on Cynthia Brewer's wonderful website www.ColorBrewer.org.

FIGURE 4.12

Whenever we need to display a range of values that has a natural breakpoint in the middle, a diverging scale handles this nicely and provides the additional benefit of more colors that can be distinguished within the range. Diverging scales are ideal for values such as profits and losses that have a breakpoint of zero, or for above- and below-average values. One thing we need to keep in mind when choosing colors for a diverging scale that we plan to present to others is that the combination of green and red won't work for most people who are colorblind. Approximately 10% of males and 0.5% of females are colorblind and the vast majority of them cannot distinguish red from green.

Comparing Spatial Values within Categories and through Time

With bar and line graphs, it is easy to compare values that are associated with a set of items in a category (e.g., bars representing sales revenues per product) or through time (e.g., a line representing sales revenues from month to month). However, comparisons of this type require special handling when values are displayed on a map. Imagine that we want to compare profits earned for the sales of five different products by state, or that we want to see how the number of influenza cases per county has changed from week to week through an entire flu season. If the values must appear on a map to reveal geographical relationships among them, it probably won't work to place five bubbles in each state to compare products or 12 bubbles per county to view the weekly pattern of change in influenza. Two solutions to this challenge are available:

- Small multiples of maps
- Deviation maps

A small-multiples display in this case would consist of a set of maps—one per item in a category (e.g., per product) or one per interval of time (e.g., per week), arranged on a screen or paper so that we can compare them to one another to see how they differ. In the example below, each row of maps represents a different product category, and each column represents a different year. Bubble size and color intensity are both being used to represent sales revenues.

FIGURE 4.13

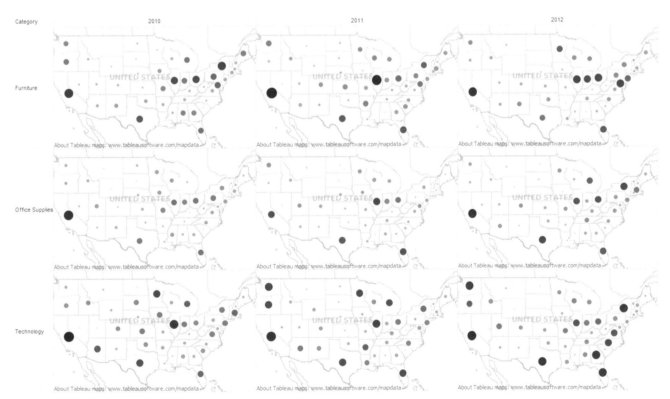

We obviously aren't going to use this display to make precise revenue comparisons, but we can use it to spot geographical differences, such as the fact that furniture sales in the contiguous states of Illinois, Indiana, and Ohio changed significantly from 2010 through 2012, featured below from left to right.

FIGURE 4.14

Let's say that we want to focus only on changes in furniture-sales revenues per state between 2010 and 2011. Rather than showing two maps side by side, one for each year, we could directly display the differences between revenues in the two years. I call these *deviation maps*. The figure below is an example.

FIGURE 4.15

In this example, the bubbles are equal in size so that they all stand out equally and exhibit only varied color intensity: blue for increases and red for decreases. Alternatively, we could use a choropleth map to display the same information, and variations in color intensity could fill entire states.

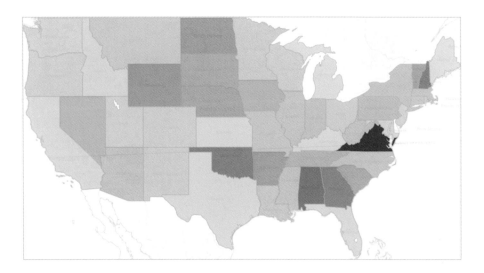

FIGURE 4.16

Deviations can be displayed directly on a map not only for comparing values that have changed through time, but also for comparing values associated with other categorical items, such as the difference in sales between two products.

Deviations are not restricted to pairs of values (e.g., two points in time or two products) but can be displayed in a series of small multiples to enable several comparisons. In the following example, three maps display changes in revenues per state from one year to the next through four years of time.

FIGURE 4.17

When deciding whether to use a map for a visualization, we need to keep the following in mind: if it's not necessary to see the *locations* of values in relation to one another in order to make the comparisons that interest us, then there are visual techniques that more clearly reveal patterns and magnitudes than maps can do. For example, we could use the series of line graphs below to show the same data that we saw in the maps above.

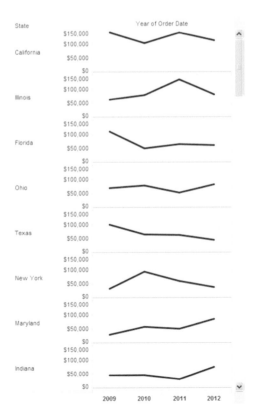

FIGURE 4.18

Now that we've covered visualizations of space in this chapter, we'll move on to the other special category that reveals more than any other: time.

Answers to questions on page 95:

1. Yes. A geospatial display would not be necessary to determine how many patrons live in low-income neighborhoods, but determining the best location for a new branch would benefit from a geospatial display.

2. No.

3. Yes. We could determine general location information about the origins of these attacks (e.g., country or origin) without a geospatial display, but a better sense of the locations of attackers, including their locations relative to one another would benefit from a geospatial display.

4. Yes. We could determine which bus routes carry the fewest passengers without a geospatial display, but we would need to see how the routes interact with one another on a geospatial display to get the full picture.

5. Yes. We could determine the regions, such as cities or postal code areas, where delivery times are poor without a geospatial display, but smaller areas such as particular neighborhoods or areas of poor delivery times that cross boundaries could not be identified without a geospatial display.

6. No.

7. Yes. Specific neighborhoods or intersections would be difficult to identify without seeing the data displayed geospatially.

8. Yes, for the same reasons as number 7.

9. No.

10. No. We could determine which rooms are hotter or colder than a specified range of temperature without a geospatial display. If we want to understand why some rooms might be hotter or colder than normal, however, a geospatial display might reveal explanatory conditions such as the position of the sun in relation to the rooms.

5   VARIATION THROUGH TIME

We have the greatest opportunity to detect signals when we examine variation through time.

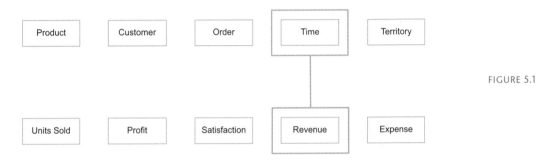

FIGURE 5.1

Variation that isn't random is, in the language of statistical process control (SPC), the result of a *special cause*. Something unusual and significant happened. If the unusual value is a problem, we will strive to control it. If it is beneficial, we will attempt to make it happen more. To do this, we need reliable ways to separate non-random changes from those that are routine.

Time-Series Relationships

Stories of quantitative change through time exhibit particular attributes, including the following:

- Trends
- Variability
- Co-variation
- Rates of change
- Cycles
- Outliers

Changes in any of these attributes are potentially meaningful. We'll focus on some more than others, but we'll examine them all as we survey the land.

A *trend* is the overall nature of change during a particular span of time. For example, during the last year did expenses tend to move up, down, or remain relatively flat? Trend is the big picture of change.

Variability is the extent to which a series of values goes up and down through time. Do revenues remain fairly steady from day to day, week to week, month to month, and quarter to quarter or do they exhibit volatility?

Co-variation refers to relationships between different sets of values in which behavior in one set is associated with corresponding behavior in the other.

Co-variation effects sometimes occur simultaneously and sometimes before (leading) or after (lagging) one another. For example, changes in customer sentiment about a particular product—either positive or negative—might show up as corresponding changes in sales of that product. Knowing these relationships can sometimes give us glimpses into the future and a degree of control over outcomes.

The *rate of change* in a variable is the speed at which it alters; this is different from the amount that the variable changes. Sales of a particular product in a large region might increase by greater amounts from month to month compared to a small region but at a slower rate. Understanding the rate of change is critical if we want to assess performance and try to anticipate the future.

Some patterns of change repeat themselves over and over in *cycles*. The number of visits to a web site might exhibit a particular pattern across the days of the week. Sales might exhibit a quarterly pattern with a peak that always occurs in the final month of the quarter, followed by a substantial drop in the first month of the next quarter. Cyclical patterns, such as those that correspond to changes in the weather, sometimes relate to seasons. Recognizing these cyclical patterns and how they evolve over time is useful.

One of the most important attributes of change through time is exceptional values—*outliers*. Values that separate themselves from the pack are sometimes indications of significant change but can also be nothing but random variation.

To become familiar with this land, we'll rely on a particular set of graphs that augment our ability to easily and clearly view change through time.

Graphs for Exploring Time Series

Almost every graph that we'll use to explore time series will represent a set of values as a line that varies vertically in position as it extends from left to right across the plot area. Nothing does a better job of showing patterns of change through time and enabling comparisons of those patterns than a simple line graph because it eliminates all but the pattern. We can use a line graph to examine each of the key attributes of change through time that are described above.

Graphs for Viewing and Comparing Trends

Trends often reveal themselves as lines that extend upward, downward, or remain relatively flat across the plot area. However, an overall trend can be masked by a great deal of variation (i.e., up and down movement). Although it is tempting to use our software tools to display a linear trend line (a.k.a., a straight line of best fit) to summarize the overall nature of change, we should avoid this practice because it can be very misleading. Let me illustrate. The following graph shows a series of monthly revenue values from October 2012 through September 2013:

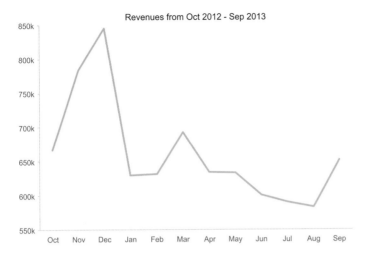

FIGURE 5.2

In the next version of the graph, I've added a black linear trend line.

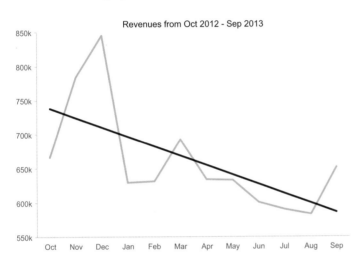

FIGURE 5.3

Most people, upon seeing this downward-sloped trend line would assume that revenues are decreasing overall to a significant degree. Even without the trend line, we can see that revenues have trended downward during this particular 12-month period. But we must be careful to not read too much into this. In the graph below, I've shown 12 months worth of revenues, this time beginning in January of the current year.

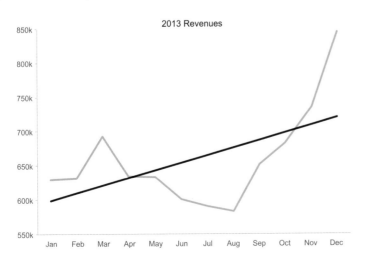

FIGURE 5.4

The trend has now completely changed direction. The overall nature of a linear trend can be excessively influenced by values at the beginning or end of the series. Therefore, when we want a sense of the overall nature of change through time, it usually works better to avoid linear trend lines and use moving averages instead. A moving (a.k.a., running) average smooths the nature of change by reducing the variation from one interval of time to the next. It does this by averaging the values of several intervals in time for each interval along the line. The example below displays a three-month moving average of revenues. Each month's value is the average of that month's actual revenue and that of the previous two months; in other words, each value along the line is the average of three consecutive months' values.

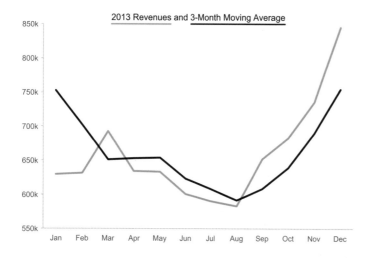

FIGURE 5.5

Although this is not as simple a picture as a linear trend line, it gives a more accurate picture of the overall nature of the change, which doesn't merely go either up or down.

Trends exhibited by multiple time series can be displayed and compared using moving averages. The following line graph is not a useful way to compare the moving averages of revenues in the U.S. and Canada. Why? Because the Canadian sales revenues are so much lower than those in the U.S. that Canada's line looks flat, hiding the patterns of change.

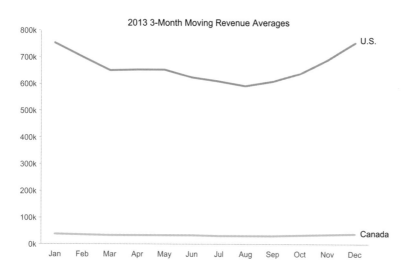

FIGURE 5.6

We can solve this problem quite simply by expressing both U.S. and Canadian sales as each month's percentage of each series' total sales. Here's the same data expressed in this manner:

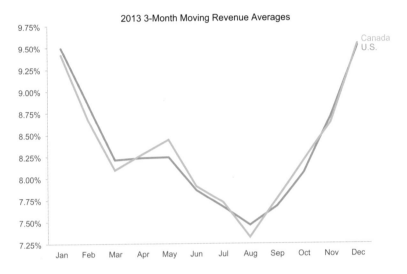

FIGURE 5.7

Now the patterns of change along both series of moving averages can be easily seen and compared. This simple trick of expressing individual time-series values as percentages of the entire series will come in handy again and again.

Graphs for Viewing and Comparing Variability

The extent and pattern of variability in a single series of values can be easily and clearly displayed in a line graph. In the example below, we can see that the values during this period vary from a low of about $510,000 to a high of a little less than $850,000, around a mean of about $660,000.

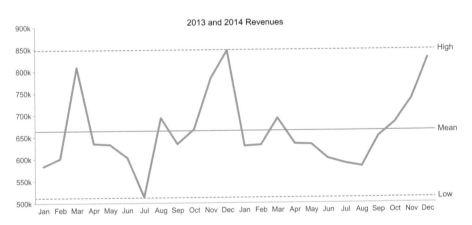

FIGURE 5.8

In addition to these basic facts, we can also see that revenues vary quite a bit from month to month.

In the following example, two lines appear: one for U.S. sales and one for Canadian sales. Which is more highly variable?

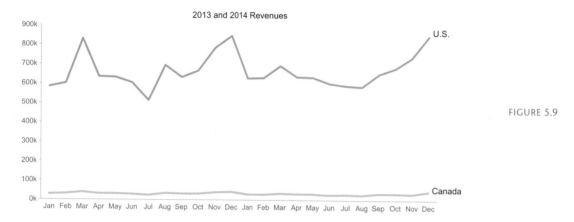

FIGURE 5.9

We can easily see that U.S. sales vary by a greater dollar amount overall and from month to month, but do they also vary by a greater percentage? We can't answer this question with this graph because a percentage variation that would appear as a large change along the U.S. revenues line would barely register along the Canadian revenues line. This is because of the significant difference between the high U.S. revenues and relatively low Canadian revenues. Once again, however, this problem can be easily solved by expressing individual time-series values as percentages of the entire series, as shown below.

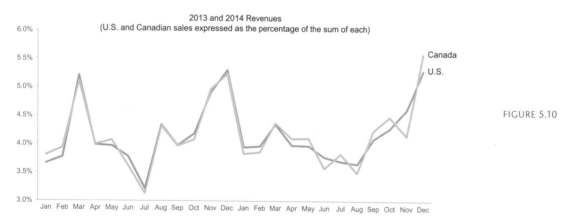

FIGURE 5.10

Now we can see that U.S sales and Canadian sales exhibit similar patterns of variation.

Graphs for Viewing and Comparing Co-variation

We can also see how multiple time series vary in relation to one another when we use the method illustrated above: expressing each time series' values as percentages of the sum for the entire period. Looking once again at the last example, we can easily see that the patterns of change in U.S. and Canadian sales through time were similar with only minor exceptions, mostly from June through November of 2014.

Graphs for Viewing and Comparing Rates of Change

Several graphical methods can be used to compares rates of change, but two in particular are quick and easy. The first involves the use of a *logarithmic scale* (a.k.a., *log scale*) along the quantitative axis. A standard linear scale along the Y axis in the graph below shows patterns of change in revenues but not their rates of change.

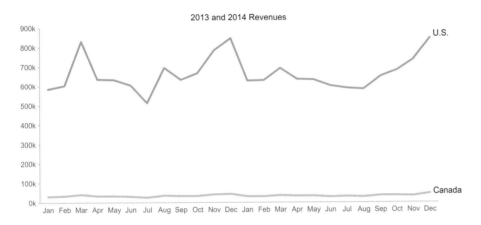

FIGURE 5.11

With a log scale, however, we could compare rates of change by simply comparing the slopes of the lines.

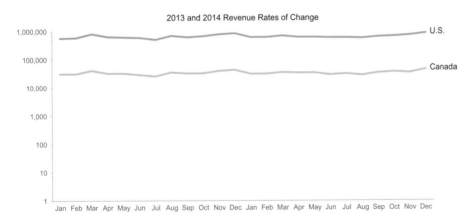

FIGURE 5.12

Equal rates of change are represented as equal slopes along the lines. Now we can see that the sales exhibit quite similar rates of change with only minor exceptions. This particular log scale has a base of 10, which means that each value along the scale is 10 times the previous value (1, 10, 100, etc.). However, equal rates of change are exhibited as equal slopes no matter what the base is.

To show the patterns of change in the rates along each line more clearly, we could narrow the scale to begin just a little below the lowest value in the data, for example at 10,000, resulting in the graph below.

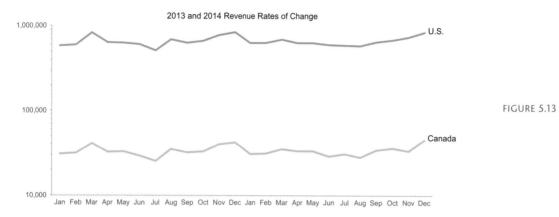

FIGURE 5.13

Even though the lines are farther apart, their patterns are now easier to see and compare, revealing subtle differences between them.

The other simple way to compare rates of change involves the common expression of all values along each series as percentage differences from the initial value of the series (in this case January 2013). In the example below, I've expressed the revenue values from the previous graphs in this manner.

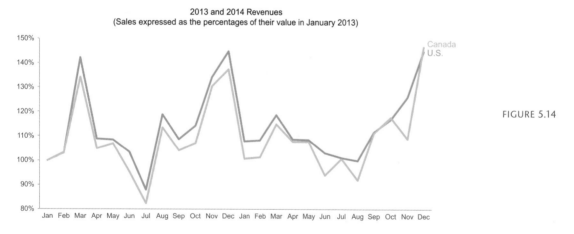

FIGURE 5.14

As we can see, slightly more work is needed to calculate the differences using this approach, but it enables more precise comparisons. We can now see that, during this two-year period, U.S. revenues increased by a greater rate than Canadian revenues in every month except October and December of 2014.

Graphs for Viewing and Comparing Cyclical Patterns

Regular line graphs work well for comparing cyclical patterns of change through time when we use a separate line for each cycle. In the following line graph, we can see that there is a typical cyclical pattern that repeats itself each year. For example, August always exhibits the lowest and September always exhibits the highest sales in each year.

FIGURE 5.15

These patterns across the months of each year are difficult to precisely compare when the series is displayed as a single line. We can address this by creating a separate line for each year, as illustrated below.

FIGURE 5.16

Now we can see that these patterns have been consistent in all three years even though sales have decreased in magnitude each year. This approach works well for comparing cyclical patterns among a few periods of time, but it doesn't excel at showing the typical cyclical pattern and how it has changed during many periods of time. For this, a special type of line graph called a *cycle plot* is useful.

William Cleveland, Douglas Dunn, and Irma Terpenning of Bell Laboratories invented the cycle plot in the 1970s. Let's learn about it one step at a time. We'll start with a standard line graph of 56 days of items sold, beginning on a Monday and ending on a Sunday. These items exhibit a cyclical pattern across the days of the week.

Cycle plots were originally introduced in:

William Cleveland, Douglas Dunn, and Irma Terpenning (1978). "The SABL Seasonal Analysis Package—Statistical and Graphical Procedures." Bell Laboratories: Computing Information Service.

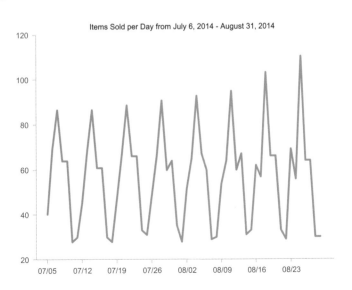

FIGURE 5.17

This continuous series of days is not the best way to view the typical cyclical pattern across the days of the week. For this view, we could show the average number of items sold for each day of the week during this 56-day period, which would look like this:

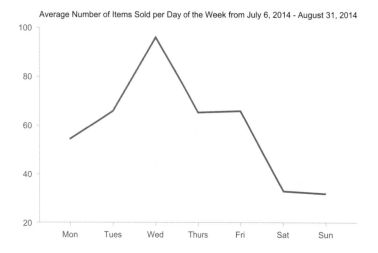

FIGURE 5.18

This summarized view shows an average weekly pattern more clearly than the previous graph but does not give us information about how this cyclical pattern might have changed during the 56-day period of time. In a single view, a cycle plot combines the typical cyclical pattern with information about the way it has changed, as illustrated below.

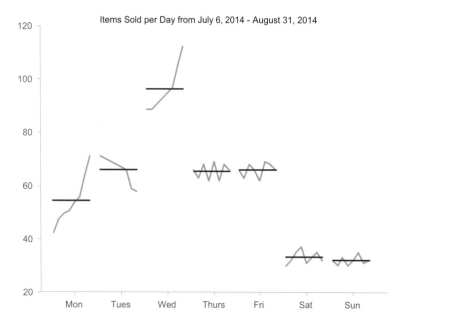

FIGURE 5.19

The horizontal gray lines display the average number of items sold for each day of the week, which summarizes the typical cyclical pattern. The green lines display the individual values for each day of the week to show how the cyclical pattern has changed during the 56-day period. With this cycle plot, we can now easily see that the pattern of items sold from Thursday through Sunday has remained fairly constant with individual values that remain near the gray horizontal line, but sales on Mondays through Wednesdays have changed significantly, with Mondays and Wednesdays consistently increasing and Tuesdays consistently decreasing.

Cycle plots are typically only found in statistical analysis products (SAS, R, etc.), but they can sometimes be created with a little effort in other products as well (e.g., in Excel and Tableau) if you know the tricks.

Graphs for Viewing Outliers

Outliers matter when they are caused by something, not when they occur randomly. Occurrences of variation in values and patterns through time that are neither routine nor random are signals. Spotting them when they occur is one of the central themes of this book. We'll examine graphs that can be used to do this in *Chapter 9 – Install Signal Sensors*.

Instructions for creating cycle plots in Excel can be found through a web search, including instructions on my own site, www.PerceptualEdge.com.

6 RELATIONSHIPS AMONG MEASURES

Previously, we examined variation within individual measures in the form of distributions. Now we'll examine the ways that individual measures can relate to one another.

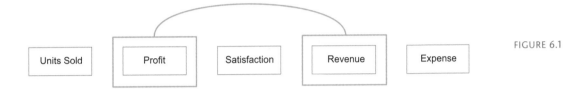

FIGURE 6.1

Quantitative Co-relationships

Relationships between quantitative variables are called *correlations* (i.e., "co-relations"). Simply stated, two variables are correlated whenever the values of one variable vary systematically with the values of the other. As it's often used by statisticians, however, the term "correlation" has a more restricted meaning, referring only to linear relationships. I've made more than a few statisticians apoplectic by using the term correlation to refer to co-relations that are not linear.

A linear correlation is one that, when viewed in a scatter plot, roughly exhibits the shape of a straight line. As the values of one variable increase, values of the other variable either increase or decrease at a consistent rate.

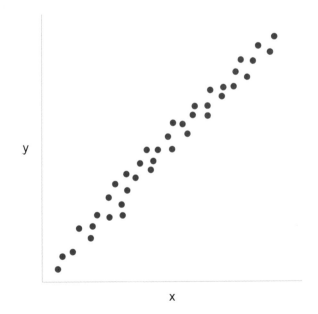

FIGURE 6.2

But what about a relationship that exhibits a consistently growing increase in variable Y for each unit of increase in variable X? In other words, increases in variable Y are *exponential*, illustrated below.

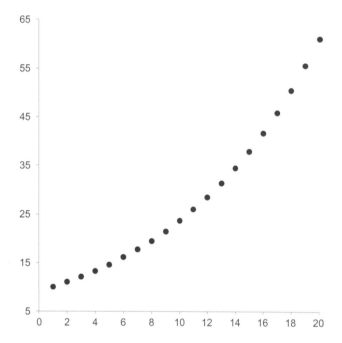

FIGURE 6.3

Is this not a correlation? Many statisticians would insist that it isn't—that it is a *relationship* but not a *correlation*. The statistical approach to this terminology stems from the fact that, just as many distribution statistics apply exclusively to normal distributions, so many correlation statistics, such as the *correlation coefficient*, apply exclusively to linear correlations. For me, the solution is to use "correlation" as the generic term for co-relationships between quantitative variables and to explicitly differentiate between *linear* and *non-linear* correlations. Problem solved. Although not everyone agrees with this use of the term, in this book we'll refer to co-relationships between quantitative variables of all shapes as "correlations."

Correlation and Causation

There is one statement that you can always count on hearing in an introductory lecture about statistical correlation: "Correlation does not necessarily indicate causation." This is an important point. Variables X and Y can be correlated, even highly so, without X *causing* the corresponding behavior that occurs in Y or vice versa. Usually, when a correlation between X and Y exists but causation isn't directly involved, it is because behaviors of both X and Y are being caused by one or more other variables. In other words, both X and Y are outcomes of another cause.

So what value is there in discovering a correlation that isn't causal in nature? Some advocates of Big Data argue that causation no longer matters. If you've identified a correlation, that's good enough; just put it to use. This argument makes those of us who've spent our lives trying to understand data queasy. Putting something to use without understanding it is a risky game. Using anabolic steroids to build large muscles before understanding the mechanism that makes the drugs work—and their possible side effects—is foolish. Advocates of Big Data who believe that technology is somehow beyond reproach and always good for us are also foolish. Here's what I think. The primary benefit of finding a correlation that isn't causal in nature is that it is a potential step on the path to finding a cause. The greatest signals in correlations are revelations of cause, which allow us to consider how we might use that understanding to do something beneficial.

Correlations abound, but most of them are useless in and of themselves. Knowing that there's a correlation between ice cream sales and drowning deaths isn't useful. Both result from warm weather. You can't stop people from drowning by shutting down ice cream parlors. Compared to the number of correlations that reside in our data, the number of causal relationships is small. According to Nate Silver, non-causal correlations are noise.

> *The number of meaningful relationships in data—those that speak to causality rather than correlation and testify to how the world really works—is orders of magnitudes smaller. Nor is it likely to be increasing at nearly so fast a rate as the information itself; there isn't any more truth in the world than there was before the Internet or the printing press. Most of the data is just noise, as most of the universe is filled with empty space.*

Nate Silver (2012). *The Signal and the Noise.* Penguin Press, page 250.

Big Data will not increase the number of meaningful relationships that exist in the world. It will only make them harder to find.

In the beginning of the previous chapter, we talked briefly about statistical process control (SPC). We cannot begin to manage processes until we've identified and understand the few key causal relationships that produce the outcomes we desire. These become the factors that we track through time and seek to use, if possible, to maintain and improve healthy processes.

Once we've identified a correlation, how do we determine whether it's causal? In his book, *Just Plain Data Analysis*, Gary Klass describes this process as it applies to social data:

> *Beginning with evidence of a relationship that supports a descriptive conclusion and then drawing a conclusion that implies causation usually requires both additional statistical evidence and a whole lot of reasoning and analysis. Data are just one part of causal arguments: no amount of empirical evidence alone is sufficient to support a claim that any social phenomenon is caused by something else. Ideally, causal claims are grounded in well-reasoned theoretical arguments and are supported by examples and illustrations in addition to the data that define the relationship.*
>
> *To discount the possibility that an observed relationship is not a causal relationship, one must assess the alternative explanations for the relationship. To be confident that an observed relationship is indeed a causal*

relationship, it is necessary to rule out the competing reasonable alternative explanations of the relationship.

If we find an observed relationship between two variables, X and Y, we can conclude that X causes Y if it is not the case that

- *There is no real relationship. This would be the case if the relationship is due to unreliable data measurement. If the observed relationship is within the bounds of sampling error, it is considered not statistically significant. Alternatively, there may be an underlying relationship, but the size of the relationship and the sample size are too small to be confident that it exists.*
- *Y causes X. Nations with the highest rates of poverty often have the highest rates of political corruption. Does corruption cause poverty, or poverty the corruption?...*
- *Something else, related to X, causes Y. When this occurs, we say that the original relationship was spurious.*

Gary M. Klass (2008). *Just Plain Data Analysis*. Rowman & Littlefield Publishers, Inc., pages 16 and 17.

In other words, to identify causal relationships, we must use our heads. No statistic can give us the answer. Statistics are only as smart as the people who use them.

Key Characteristics of Correlations

The nature of a correlation can be summarized by three key characteristics:

- Strength
- Direction
- Shape

The strength of a correlation is the degree to which values of one variable inform us about the corresponding values of another variable. A perfect correlation—one that's as strong as possible—grants us precise knowledge of one variable based on knowledge of another. If there were a perfect correlation between the height and weight of people, then, if I measured your height, I could tell you your weight. Obviously, the correlation between height and weight is less than perfect. The most common statistical measure of a correlation's strength is the *correlation coefficient*, but this only applies to linear correlations. Its values range from -1.0 to +1.0 because, in addition to a linear correlation's strength, the correlation coefficient also identifies its direction: positive values for positive correlations and negative values for negative correlations. We'll get to a correlation's direction in a moment. The closer a value comes to either +1 or -1 (i.e., the farther it is from 0), the stronger the correlation. In his book *Statistics in Plain English*, Timothy Urdan, a statistician who works in the social sciences, describes the nature of correlation coefficients:

Perfect correlations are never found in actual social science research. Generally, correlation coefficients stay between -.70 and +.70. Some textbook authors suggest that correlation coefficients between -.20 and +.20 indicate a weak relation between two variables, those between .20 and .50 (either positive or negative) represent a moderate relationship, and those larger than .50 (either positive or negative) represent a strong relationship. These general rules of thumb for judging the relevance of correlation coefficients must be taken with a grain of salt. For example, even a "small" correlation between alcohol consumption and liver disease (e.g., +.15) is important, whereas a strong correlation between how much children like vanilla and chocolate ice cream (e.g., +.70) may not be so important.

Timothy C. Urdan (2010). *Statistics in Plain English*, Third Edition. Routledge, page 80.

Once again, we're reminded that we must use our heads. A statistical measure of a correlation's strength is handy and useful, but what it means will always depend on context.

The direction of a correlation is easy to determine when the correlation is linear in nature. As the value of X increases, the value of Y either increases (positive) or decreases (negative). When we examine data in a scatter plot, we can determine simply by looking whether a linear correlation is positive or negative, assuming that it exists and isn't terribly weak. As illustrated in the example below, when the values are sloped upward from left to right, the correlation is positive, and when they're sloped downward, it's negative.

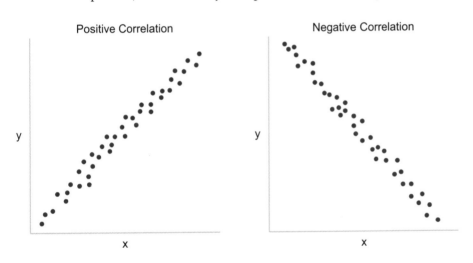

FIGURE 6.4

Even when correlations aren't linear, they still usually have a direction. For example, even though the correlation in the example below is curved in an "S" shape, called a *logistic curve*, it's still positive because it never goes downward as it moves from left to right.

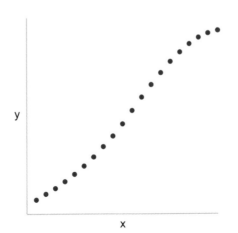

FIGURE 6.5

Where things get a little tricky is when the shape of the correlation changes direction. In the example below, the correlation starts off positive but eventually changes direction and becomes negative.

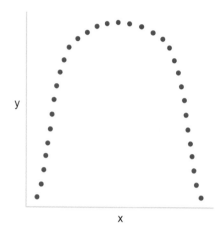

FIGURE 6.6

Imagine that this a correlation between the number of marketing emails that we send to customers and customer satisfaction based on a survey. In this case, more emails result in greater satisfaction up to a point, but beyond that threshold customers become annoyed by the emails, which causes them to avoid us. A correlation that moves in two directions cannot be accurately described by a correlation coefficient. It's important that we look at a correlation to see its shape before trusting statistical measures that assume linearity.

The shape of a correlation, which we've already touched on briefly, is the third key characteristic. Different shapes tell us different stories about the nature of the correlation or lack thereof. Therefore, we need ways to see the basic shape of a correlation even in the midst of a great deal of clutter. A simple visual summary of the correlation's shape is invaluable; we'll get to that in a minute when we talk about *fit models*. We'll see that shape is easiest to view when it is summarized by a simple line or curve that is drawn from left to right to trace the pattern among the values. But first, let's examine the three key characteristics of correlations graphically. The primary graph for viewing correlations is the *scatter plot*.

Scatter Plots for Examining Correlations

The scatter plot was invented specifically for examining correlations (or the lack thereof) between two quantitative variables. It's brilliant in the way that it displays relationships between two paired sets of values using horizontal position along the X axis for one variable and vertical position along the Y axis for the other. The following example illustrates how a single data point represents two values: one on the X axis and one on the Y axis.

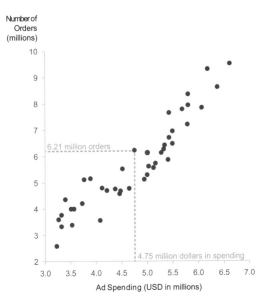

FIGURE 6.7

This arrangement makes relationships between quantitative variables readily accessible to our brains, which are well designed for perceiving 2-D positions and 2-D patterns. If you've had little or no experience with scatter plots, take the time to read about them and a few best practices for their use in my book *Now You See It.*

In the following sections, we'll look at ways to summarize the basic shape of a correlation in a scatter plot, but, for the moment, we should appreciate the usefulness of this graph as a starting view. We want to begin by viewing all of the values before we reduce the view to a summarized pattern. If we skipped immediately to a summarized view, we might miss some critical part of the correlation's story.

Important information about a correlation often exists in the details of its shape that could no longer be seen if we reduced it to a simpler, summarized representation. In addition to a correlation's overall shape, we also care about particular aspects of shape, such as gaps—places where no values appear but it seems like they should—and clusters of various sizes and densities. In the example below, the basic shape of the correlation is linear and positive, but there is a gap in the middle, with a more dispersed cluster on the left and a smaller, denser cluster on the right.

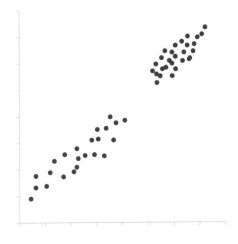

FIGURE 6.8

There's one final but important characteristic that we should look for when examining correlations visually: the presence of outliers. They're usually easy to spot because they stand apart from the others. Chances are, however, that when we examined variation within measures individually, we already saw most of the outliers that would show up in a scatter plot. In the scatter plot below, notice the lone value that stands out on the left.

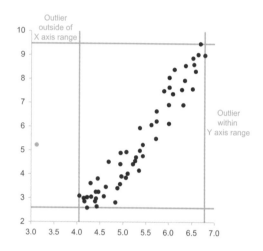

FIGURE 6.9

This value falls within the routine range of values along the Y axis but below the routine range along the X axis. This is an outlier that would have shown up when we examined the distribution of the variable on the X axis. Therefore, we can ignore it here because it's already known. We refer to this as a *univariate* (single-variable) outlier because it is only unusual relative to one variable, not both.

In the next scatter plot, notice that the outlier falls within the routine of values on each axis but stands out because it is an unusual combination of X and Y values.

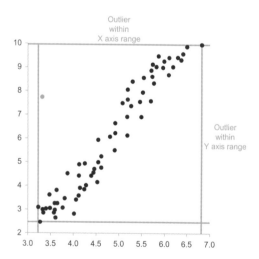

FIGURE 6.10

This is an example of a *bivariate* (two-variable) outlier: one that only qualifies as an outlier when the two variables are combined. This is new information that would not have shown up when examining distributions. If we were investigating causes of obesity, it would be worth our time to find out if this unusual combination of X and Y values is a result of a special cause.

After investigating outliers, we'll go on in the next section to look at models that describe the nature of correlations as a whole. We'll find that outliers, because they don't fit the pattern of the correlation, can make it difficult to summarize the correlation as a whole. Hartwig and Dearing suggest a way to handle this:

> *The easiest and most reasonable way to handle relationships such as [those distorted by outliers] is to separate the outliers from the rest of the data. The outliers can then be analyzed separately and the remaining cases analyzed and summarized in terms of the shape, strength, and direction of the relationship that exists among them. This is an entirely reasonable way to proceed since the outliers are, by definition, not part of the same relationship as the other cases.*

Frederick Hartwig with Brian E. Dearing (1979). *Exploratory Data Analysis.* Sage Publications, page 47.

Notice that Hartwig and Dearing didn't say that we should discard the outliers. Instead, they said that we should examine outliers separately from the rest of the data. We'll consider ways to examine both.

Summarizing Correlations with Lines or Curves

To summarize the basic shape of a correlation, we build models. These models, called *fit models* or *models of best fit*, attempt to fit lines (either straight or curved) to the overall shape of the relationship that exists between the two variables. A line can trace the shape of the data in the simplest possible way, making it easy to see, understand, and remember a pattern of correlation. We won't rely on our eyes alone to do this, however, even when the pattern seems obvious. When visualized in a graph, the structure of the correlation takes on the shape of a line, either straight or curved.

Why do we need to summarize the correlation's structure? Here's Howard Wainer's answer:

> *Data points usually contain a mixture of signal to noise. Our perceptions are often aided if there is a way to filter some of the noise and present a purer visual version of the signal. One way to do this has traditionally been smoothing, and many effective smoothers have been developed.*

Howard Wainer (2005). *Graphic Discovery: A Trout in the Milk and Other Visual Adventures.* Princeton University Press, page 138.

Wainer's explanation ties in beautifully with our objective of signal detection. The term *smoothing* is a synonym for *fitting*. Statisticians sometimes speak about the *smooth* and the *rough*: the "smooth" is another term for the "fit model," which describes the essential correlation between the variables; the "rough" consists of values that don't fit the model because they're unusual. "The smooth in a relationship is the line around which the data points in a relationship are distributed, as well as the one line which best describes the relationship" Hartwig and Dearing offer a simple equation to describe the data in a scatter plot:

> *Data = smooth + rough…*
>
> *Since the data will almost never conform exactly to the smooth, the smooth must be extracted from the data. What is left behind is the rough, the deviations from the smooth, the difference between the smooth and the*

Frederick Hartwig with Brian E. Dearing (1979). *Exploratory Data Analysis.* Sage Publications, page 37.

observed data points. What is desirable is a rough that has no smooth; that is, the rough should contain no additional pattern or structure. If the rough does contain additional structure not removed by the smooth, it is not rough enough and further smoothing should take place.

Ibid., pages 10-11.

Residual—what's left over—is another term for the rough, so the equation above can also be expressed as "data = fit model + residual." If we examine residuals and find structure in them, this tells us that our fit model can be improved to take that remaining structure into account. This is a process that sometimes requires a sequence of smoothing iterations, each getting us closer to the best fit.

> *The iterative and interactive interplay of summarizing by fit and exposing by residuals is vital to effective data analysis. Summarizing and exposing are complementary and pervasive.*

John W. Tukey and M. B. Wilk (1965). "Proceedings of the Symposium on Information Processing in Sight Sensory Systems." California Institute of Technology, page 6.

A fit model can always be explained in mathematical terms. The specific mathematical method that we use to create the fit model depends on the shape of the correlation: linear (straight) or non-linear (curved). A *straight line of best fit* (linear fit model) is also called a *least-squares regression line*. Don't let this statistical nomenclature frighten you. Essentially, the mathematical method known as least-squares regression draws a straight line in a scatter plot from left to right through the middle of the values in a manner that reduces the sum of the residuals (i.e., the distances between the values and the line) to the least amount. The residuals are then squared to convert negative values into positive values (multiplying a negative number by itself results in a positive number), which removes the unnecessary distinction between positive and negative values (it doesn't matter which side of the line the residuals fall on—only how far from the line they fall).

A regression line can be fully described by two numbers: its *slope* and its *intercept*. The slope is the degree to which values of the Y axis variable change for each unit of change in the X axis variable. For example, if we examine the correlation between women's heights in inches (X) and their weights in pounds (Y), a slope of five would indicate that for every increase in height of one inch, weight increases by five pounds. The regression line below has a slope of 4.64.

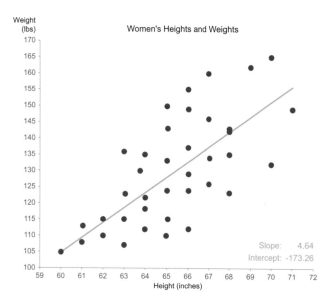

FIGURE 6.11

The intercept (a.k.a., *Y intercept*) is the corresponding value of Y for a value of X equal to zero. In other words, in a scatter plot of these two variables, at what value does the regression line cross (i.e., intercept) the Y axis for a value of zero on the X axis? In this example, the intercept is a value of -173.26. In the figure below, I've extended the scales to include the X axis value of 0 and the corresponding Y axis value of -173.26, to illustrate this more clearly.

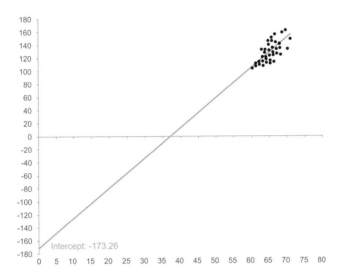

FIGURE 6.12

Of course, a weight of -173 pounds is not possible, no matter how disciplined a diet one follows!

Resistance is Not Futile

When we examined variation within measures, we found that some statistical measures of distribution are very susceptible to the influence of outliers. This is especially true of the mean as a measure of center and of measures that rely on the mean, such as the standard deviation. When outliers are present, they pull the mean in their direction, causing it to be higher or lower than it should be as a reliable measure of center. Statistical measures that are not influenced by outliers are *resistant*. They hold fast, not drawn in the direction of the outliers.

Now that we're dealing with correlations rather than distributions, we must still be concerned with resistance. We don't want the lines or curves of our fit models to be pulled in one direction or the other by outliers because outliers are unusual and therefore don't represent the essential relationship between the variables. The least-squares regression line is highly susceptible to the influence of outliers. This is because it's based on a mean. Fortunately, we can turn to other fit models to solve this problem. These alternatives typically replace means with medians to make the fit line resistant to outliers.

The *Tukey line* is an alternative for correlations that are linear (straight, not curved) in shape. It divides the values in a scatter plot into three groups—the leftmost third, the middle third, and the rightmost third—and separately calculates the medians in each group of X values and Y values; then, it uses the those medians to position the line. Back when data analysts routinely calculated statistics manually or with the help of only an electronic calculator, no one thought twice about doing the work involved in calculating something like a Tukey line. Now that we rely on software to do this for us, we're no longer willing to do this the old-fashioned way. So, if you're using software that will calculate a Tukey line for you, go for it. If not, consider the following alternative: remove the outliers from the scatter plot and then rely on a standard regression line that's built into every data analysis product available. It would be great if we could just ask the software to ignore the outliers when calculating the regression line, but that's typically not an option.

Similar to a regression line, most standard approaches to fit modeling for non-linear correlations—including logarithmic, exponential, and polynomial fit models—also lack resistance. This problem can be eliminated by removing the outliers, but we don't want to lose sight of them if we can help it. Another approach, the *locally weighted regression*, usually referred to as *lowess* or *loess*, can be used to fit non-linear relationships in a way that is more resistant to outliers. William Cleveland initially proposed the loess model in 1979. If you use software that supports the loess model, you're in luck. To learn how it works and how to use it correctly, I recommend that you read Cleveland's book *The Elements of Graphing Data*.

The goal when using a loess model is to make the smoothing parameter as large as possible, resulting in a curve that is as smooth as possible, without failing to represent any significant features of the underlying pattern. But how much curviness vs. smoothness is ideal? The curviest model possible would produce a line that precisely intersects each value in the scatter plot from left to right, which would perfectly describe the relationship between the two variables based on that specific set of values but would utterly fail to summarize the essential and generalizable relationship between the variables.

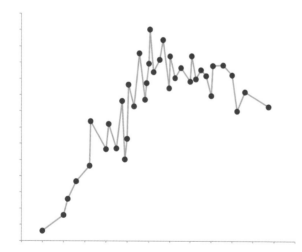

FIGURE 6.13

A model that intersects each data point would consist mostly of noise in the form of random variation. Creating a fit model that includes noise is called *overfitting*. In contrast, it is called *underfitting* when a model fails to represent the essential structure of the correlation, illustrated by the linear fit model on the following page.

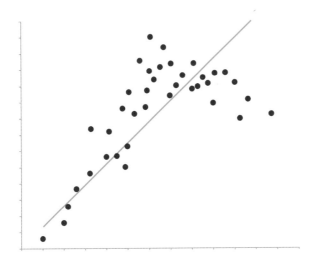

FIGURE 6.14

When using a non-linear fit model, such as a polynomial model, it is sometimes necessary to adjust its degree of curviness to find a compromise between underfitting and overfitting.

Curvy Models

We've already considered the fact that fit models can be either linear or non-linear. Non-linear models can be further distinguished as those that are *monotonic* (either positive or negative in direction but not both) or *non-monotonic* (both positive and negative in direction).

Monotonic models can have many bends but always move in the same direction, either up or down. In the example below, the curve is always positive.

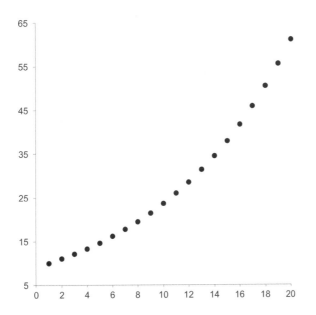

FIGURE 6.15

Something else is going on in this example besides always curving in the positive direction. This curve is also increasing more and more from one value to the next along the Y axis. The farther that we trace the line to the right, the more it curves upward. This is called an *exponential curve*. Exponential curves can either grow or decay at an exponential rate. The following example of a negative correlation decays exponentially.

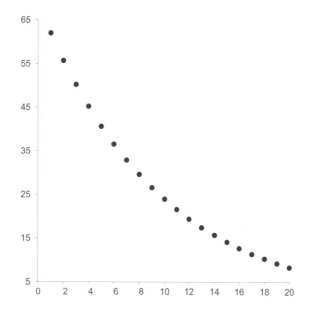

FIGURE 6.16

Now notice that the two examples below behave differently than exponential curves.

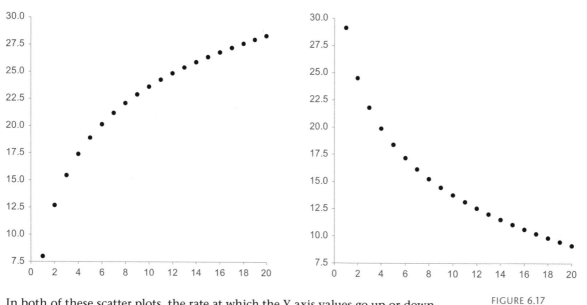

FIGURE 6.17

In both of these scatter plots, the rate at which the Y axis values go up or down decreases from left to right. These are *logarithmic curves*. Our perception of an increase in a sound's volume versus the actual change in the sound's intensity works in this way. A ten-times increase in sound intensity results in roughly a two-times increase in perceived loudness. If we displayed this correlation in a scatter plot with sound intensity on the X axis and perceived volume on the Y axis, a ten-times increase in value along the X axis would roughly correspond to a two-times increase along the Y axis.

Positive exponential and logarithmic curves behave in oppose ways. With exponential curves, increases in value along the X axis exhibit consistently greater increases in value along the Y axis; with logarithmic curves, increases in value along the X axis exhibit consistently lesser increases in value along the Y axis.

Sometimes we'll see patterns of correlation where the Y values start out changing exponentially, then switch to changing logarithmically. This is called a *logistic curve*, illustrated below.

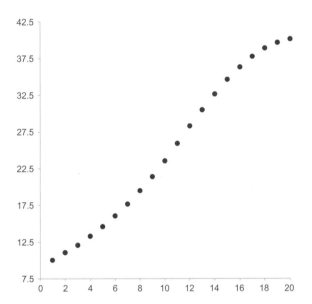

FIGURE 6.18

Product sales often exhibit this pattern because they increase rapidly during the product's youth, but the market eventually becomes saturated, and the product loses popularity as a result of competition, so sales thereafter increase at a lesser and lesser rate. Eventually, if we continued to track the product's sales, the curve would likely change direction and begin to decrease, which would make it non-monotonic.

It is essential that non-linear correlations be modeled with curves that fit their shape, whatever that shape might be. The shape of the model tells much of a correlation's story.

Transformations

In *Chapter 3 – Variation within Measures*, we touched on the occasional usefulness of transforming values to normalize a distribution's shape. Statisticians often transform values when viewing correlations in scatter plots as well, usually to make the shape of the relationship linear. Although this is useful at times, we should approach transformations with caution.

> *Transformation, even when it is done correctly and when it brings benefits,*
> *can also bring a disadvantage. With a few exceptions...re-expression moves*
> *us into a scale that is often less familiar. As a result, when we move to a*
> *new scale, we may lose some of our intuitive understanding and our ability*

to make interpretations. Such disadvantages may be of greater concern to the consumers of the analysis than to the analysts. But for most of us it is easier to think in terms of dollars, inches, or years, than it is to consider log-dollars, square-root inches, or one-over-years. Thus when we consider transformation, we should ask whether the benefits justify the effort needed and the inconvenience that may result for our consumer.

Hoaglin, Mosteller & Tukey, editors (1983). *Understanding Robust and Exploratory Data Analysis.* John Wiley & Sons, page 124.

Despite this warning, Hoaglin, Mosteller, and Tukey endorse transformations (re-expressions) when they're useful.

Re-expression involves finding what scale (e.g., logarithmic or square root) would simplify the analysis of the data. Exploratory data analysis empha-sizes the benefits of considering, at an early stage, whether the original scale of measurement for the data is satisfactory. If not, a re-expression into another scale may help to promote symmetry, constancy of variability, straightness of relationship, or additivity of effect, depending on the structure of the data.

Ibid., pages 2-3.

We always begin by examining the values in a scatter plot without transforma-tion. If we can see the nature of the relationship, we don't need to transform the values. But if the data points are clumped together in ways that make the nature of the relationship difficult to discern, a transformation might be useful.

Transformations can get quite complicated, but simple transformations are usually sufficient. The typical approach involves first looking at the distributions of each variable and transforming the values of variables that are skewed in shape to make them normal. To do this, we can use transformations that change the distances between values (e.g., logarithmic and square root) to move the peak of the distribution toward the middle, as discussed previously. We won't venture farther into this territory where the methods get complicated and the risk of error becomes great. If you have a hearty appetite for more, I recommend that you read *Exploratory Data Analysis* by Hartwig and Dearing.

Regression Analysis

So far we've kept matters relatively straightforward by limiting ourselves to correlations between two quantitative variables (bivariate correlations). To fully understand the nature of correlations in the real world, however, we must be willing to example relationships between more than two variables. To do this, we must learn a bit about *regression analysis*. WAIT! Please don't close the book just yet. I promise that our brief look at this topic won't lead to ulcers.

Regression analysis is the process of measuring relationships between vari-ables to produce an equation that can be used to predict an outcome based on a particular set of input values for those variables. The variable that's associated with the outcome is called the *dependent variable*, and those that are associated with inputs are called *independent variables*. Regression can help us answer questions as simple as how many steps a person of a particular height must take to walk a mile or as complex as what factors contribute to high scores on the

Scholastic Aptitude Test (SAT), including the proportional contributions of each. Andrew Vickers breaks this down for us:

Here is what you need to know about regression: it is just about x and y. As in y = average temperature; x is months away from summer; y = 70 – 10x...One way of thinking about this is "give me a value for x and I'll work out y for you." In other words:

- *y is something we don't know and want to predict.*
- *x is the information we have.*
- *The equation tells us how to work out y from x.*

What regression does is work out what the equation should be. Keep saying to yourself "regression gives you an equation" and it will all seem a lot more manageable.

Andrew Vickers (2010). *What is a p-value anyway?* Addison-Wesley, pages 78-79.

That's not so bad. The concept itself is fairly straightforward. The process of doing regression analysis, however, can get rather complicated. Vickers goes on to provide a simple example. He is hoping to run the New York marathon, and he wants to figure out how long it will likely take him. He decides that one way to do this is to start with the mean time that it takes people in general to run a marathon, which is 245 minutes. So far, he has the equation $y = 245$, but this is an extremely rough estimate. He then looks up the fact that, on average, women run a marathon in 263 minutes, and, on average, men do it in 239 minutes: a difference of 24 minutes. This new information can serve as an x value—an independent variable or input—to help him determine a more accurate value for y. Now that he knows that it takes women 24 more minutes than men on average, and that men run the marathon in 239 minutes on average, he can construct a regression formula: $y = 24x + 239$, where $x = 1$ for women and 0 for men. So far, this is called a *univariate regression* because it includes only one independent variable. To predict how long it will take the typical woman to run a marathon, he can assign a value of 1 to x and calculate the result as 239 minutes + (24 minutes x 1) = 263 minutes. Using the same approach he can predict his time as 239 + (24 x 0) = 239. If gender alone could be used as a reliable predictor of running time, he could stick with this simple regression. Unfortunately, gender alone is not a good predictor of marathon times. To come up with a better regression, he will need to factor in other independent variables in addition to his first variable gender (x_1); these other variables could include the person's age (x_2) and the number of training miles the person runs per week (x_3) and would produce a *multivariable regression*. Eventually, after more thought and some data analysis, Vickers produced the following regression:

y	marathon running time equals
x_1	23 times 1 for a woman or 0 for a man
x_2	plus 0.81 times the person's age
x_3	minus 1.57 times the number of training miles run a week plus 262

Voilà, he has a multivariate regression that can be used to predict marathon running times. Here's an example of how this regression would work for determining the time it would take a 48-year-old woman who runs 40 training miles a week to run a marathon:

x_1 23 times 1
x_2 plus 0.81 times 48 years old
x_3 minus 1.57 times the 40 miles run a week plus 262

y equals a marathon running time of 261 minutes

Software can easily express multivariate relationships more complex than this in the form of a regression as long as we have access to the right data. Contrary to the Big Data notion of examining every variable imaginable to produce these regressions, this process works best when directed by smart choices. The regression process proceeds as a series of thoughtful steps.

> *The typical cycle of analysis is this: The analyst evaluates the evidence to select the term that best explains the dependent variable. Then the analyst tests that term. If the result is an improvement, the variable or term is left in the equation, but if...not, the analyst may drop it and look at the displays for a new hint.*

Forrest W. Young, Pedro M. Valero-Mora, and Michael Friendly (2006). *Visual Statistics*. Wiley, page 68.

My goals here are to explain what regression analysis is and to assure us that, with the help of good software and a good book or two, it's within our reach. To venture into this territory successfully, however, we'll need to develop a few new skills. The wise choices that drive this process toward success don't come naturally; they are the result of training and practice. I recommend starting this process by reading *Naked Statistics* by Charles Wheelan.

Only one of the six fundamental types of variation and relationships remains: relationships among categories. We'll look at it in the next chapter.

7 RELATIONSHIPS AMONG CATEGORIES

Examining relationships among categories extends the information that we learned in Chapter 2 when we examined variation within categories. Now, rather than looking for the ways that items within a category relate to one another based on a particular measure (e.g., how individual products contribute proportionally to total revenue), we'll add more categories to the mix.

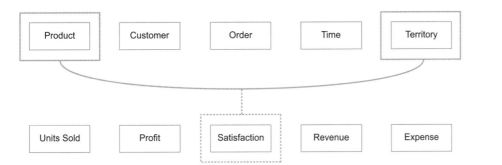

FIGURE 7.1

Visual Crosstabs

It was primarily for the purpose of examining relationships among categories that *pivot tables*, also called *crosstabs*, were invented around 20 years ago. A pivot table allows us to see values at the intersections of categories. The example below makes it easy for us to look up the amount of sales revenue that's associated with each possible intersection of product sub-category and region.

	Region			
Product Type	Central	West	East	South
Office Machines	$563,395	$673,390	$321,105	$610,807
Tables	$471,751	$454,887	$652,965	$316,405
Telephones and Communication	$613,410	$475,653	$394,726	$405,524
Chairs & Chairmats	$651,654	$348,052	$469,652	$292,478
Copiers and Fax	$404,175	$343,117	$173,833	$209,237
Storage & Organization	$299,116	$227,534	$280,367	$263,166
Binders and Binder Accessories	$309,262	$203,847	$294,907	$214,942
Bookcases	$258,919	$246,411	$145,818	$171,504
Computer Peripherals	$250,718	$150,974	$198,649	$195,535
Appliances	$317,079	$133,946	$136,944	$149,023
Office Furnishings	$259,389	$159,443	$149,828	$129,434
Paper	$150,710	$98,576	$96,958	$100,210
Envelopes	$47,531	$49,608	$43,691	$33,256
Pens & Art Supplies	$45,807	$42,625	$42,908	$35,768
Scissors, Rulers and Trimmers	$36,376	$30,577	$4,729	$9,315
Labels	$14,062	$7,692	$6,298	$10,930
Rubber Bands	$5,815	$3,416	$3,089	$2,687

FIGURE 7.2

These powerful tables allow us to easily answer important questions, such as:

- How do specific products relate to specific regions based on revenues?
- How do specific customers relate to specific shipping methods based on the order count?
- How do specific diseases relate to specific racial groups based on the number of cases per 1,000 people?
- What particular combination of customer type, location, product type, and sales channel represents our highest profits?

Pivot tables that display numbers, such as the one above, are great for looking up specific values, but they aren't particularly good for comparing many values or for seeing the overall pattern in a series of values. For these purposes, we need graphs. It was for this reason that, about 10 years ago, software products began to extend the crosstab arrangement of data into the graphical realm as *visual crosstabs*. Here's the same data that we saw in the traditional pivot table on the previous page, now displayed graphically:

Tableau Software was the first company to make visual crosstabs readily available and easy to use.

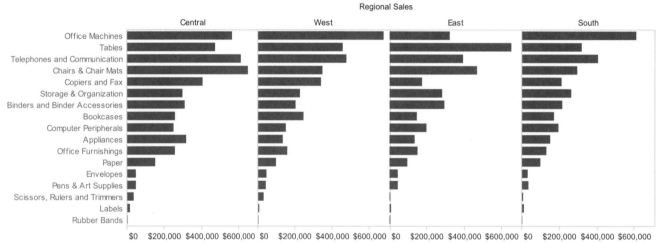

FIGURE 7.3

Many features that weren't noticeable in the pivot table are now easy to see. For example, the following four features caught my attention almost immediately:

- The highest revenues are associated with the sale of Office Machines in the West.
- Although Office Machines sell the most overall, in the Central and East regions other product sub-categories sell better.
- Sales of office machines in the East are much less than elsewhere.
- The five product sub-categories with the lowest sales overall also have the lowest sales in each of the four regions.

Small multiples, arranged as a visual crosstab, are the primary visualization technique that we'll use for examining relationships among categories.

Visual crosstabs can be easily enriched to place even more information before our eyes at once. For instance, we can examine relationships among categories based on more than one measure at a time. In the following example, we can see relationships between product sub-categories and regions based on both revenues and profits.

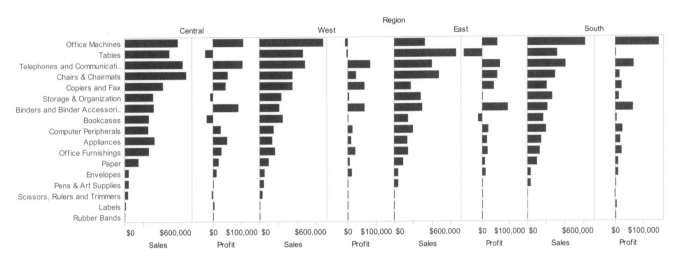

FIGURE 7.4

Knowing that the product sub-categories have been sorted from highest to lowest sales revenues across all regions, we can now see that the second product sub-category—Tables—sells well but loses money or barely breaks even in every region.

We can continue to enrich the display by adding more information as long as each new addition is displayed simply and clearly in a way that works for our eyes and brains. For example, to focus on the correlation between revenues and profit (or lack thereof), we could switch to the visual crosstab below:

FIGURE 7.5

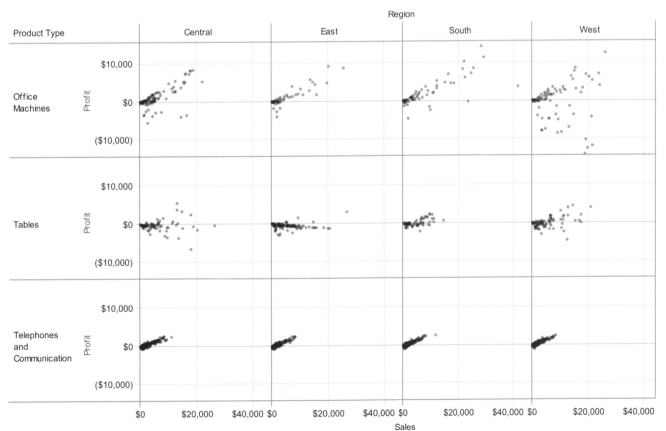

In this case, a measure isn't mediating the relationship between two categories but instead a relationship between two measures (sales and profits).

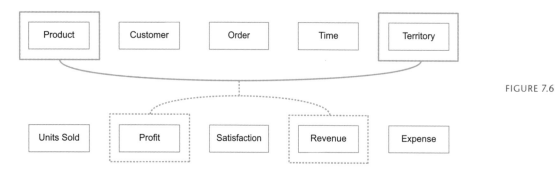

FIGURE 7.6

Each data point in the scatter plots represents the revenue and profit associated with an individual order. Looking at the top four product sub-categories (the only sub-categories visible in this example), we can see that the positive correlation that usually exists between revenues and profits does not hold true for Office Machines in the West (the scatter plot in the upper right corner). It's unlikely that we would have become aware of this relationship between product sub-categories and regions without a visual crosstab display.

We've now covered the individual types of variation within variables and relationships among them that make up our survey of the land. However, before moving on to discuss signal detection, we need to bring these individual ways of viewing data together into richer, multi-perspective views. Only then can all of the meaningful connections be seen. That's the topic of our next chapter.

8 RELATIONSHIPS AMONG MULTIPLE PERSPECTIVES AND VARIABLES

When we began our journey, we headed first for high ground to get an overview of the land. Since then, we've moved between high ground and expeditions into the forests—the big picture and the details—to build a comprehensive understanding of the land. We stood on the summit with the entire land stretched out before us, and then explored it, one type of data analysis, one feature, at a time. Each feature of the land, each type of analysis, required special lenses for discovery and examination. We've learned a great deal, but our understanding isn't complete. It remains fragmented. It's time to bring things together.

Multi-perspective Views

We can't fully understand the land if we allow the six essential types of data analysis that we've learned to remain disconnected from one another. So far, we've focused on one perspective at a time. Now we need to consider multiple perspectives at once. Many insights are lodged in crevasses and only come to light when we examine the land from several perspectives simultaneously. By viewing the land from several perspectives at once, we'll discover that the curvy road, which seemed so odd when examined alone, takes its shape from a meandering river that flows next to it. We'll learn that some trees grow only at particular elevations and only on hillsides that face in one direction.

When we look at the object below, we see a circle.

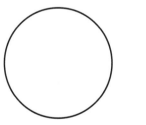

FIGURE 8.1

And when we look at the next object, we see a square.

FIGURE 8.2

It isn't obvious, however, that both images above show the same object seen from different perspectives.

Here it is again viewed from a third perspective.

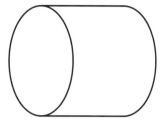

FIGURE 8.3

When we see something from a single perspective only, we often misunderstand it. To fully understand something, we must view it from every perspective.

I was once told by someone who claimed to understand the art of Picasso that Picasso's cubist work was an attempt to incorporate several views of an object, each from a different perspective, into a single image. Imagine a well-lighted studio with a nude woman holding a mandolin in the center of the room and five painters positioned at various locations around her. Each artist paints an image from his unique perspective. Now imagine that Picasso comes along and combines those five perspectives into a single painting.

Figure 8.4

Pablo Picasso (1910). "Girl Playing Mandolin."

No wonder cubist paintings are disorienting.

Let's switch from multi-perspective paintings to a computer screen on which we can simultaneously view a data set from several perspectives. For data sensemaking purposes, these different perspectives must be presented in a way that makes it possible for our brains to combine them into an understanding of the whole. No matter how much we might admire the brilliance and beauty of Picasso's work, we won't take a cubist approach to the visualization! Let's find a multi-perspective representation of data that works more straightforwardly for our brains.

The Porsches in the bird's-eye photo below serve as a small multiples' display of sorts. Each car is a different model.

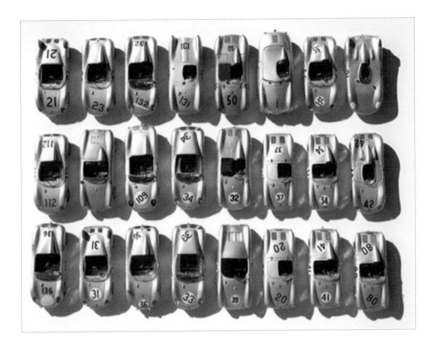

FIGURE 8.5

With this photo, we can compare these models, but only from a single perspective: from above, looking down. Instead of many categorical slices viewed from a single perspective, what if we want to view these cars from multiple perspectives simultaneously? In other words, we need a view such as the following:

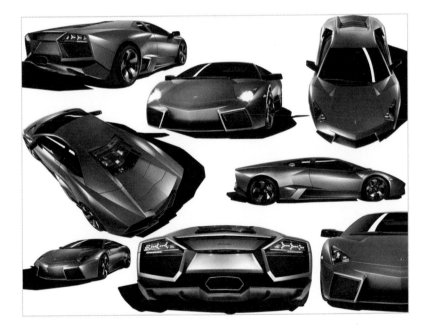

FIGURE 8.6

Image source: Steve Calderon.

Seeing all of these independent perspectives arranged before our eyes at the same time allows us to get a better sense of the car as a whole than we could get by viewing each of these perspectives separately.

Now imagine that we're analyzing sales data. During the course of the journey so far, we've learned a great deal from individual views of sales activity. We've seen how revenues and profits vary by product category and region:

We've seen how base product margins are distributed across the quantitative range:

FIGURE 8.7

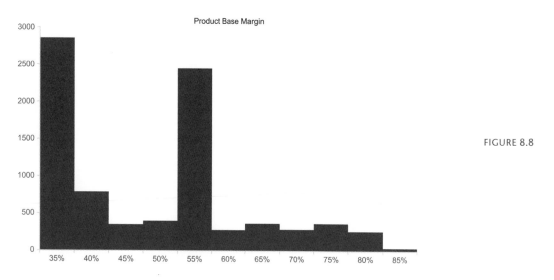

FIGURE 8.8

We've seen how revenues (bubble size) and profits (bubble color intensity) vary geographically:

FIGURE 8.9

We've seen how revenues vary through time by region and product category:

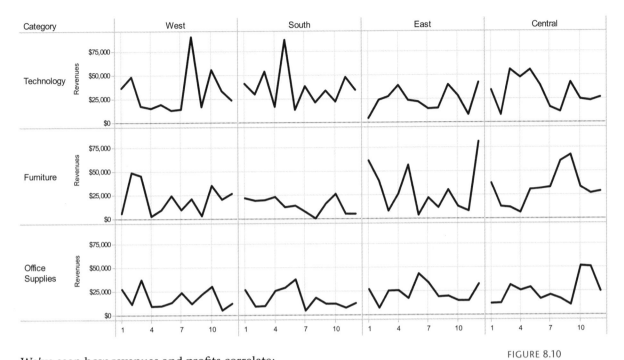

FIGURE 8.10

We've seen how revenues and profits correlate:

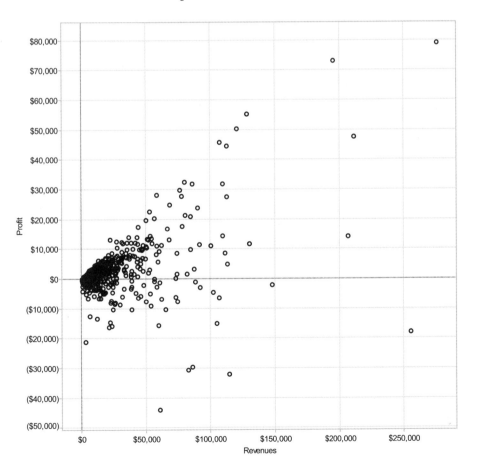

FIGURE 8.11

Now, to understand these relationships more holistically, it would be useful to place these views together, all before our eyes simultaneously. The following display does this:

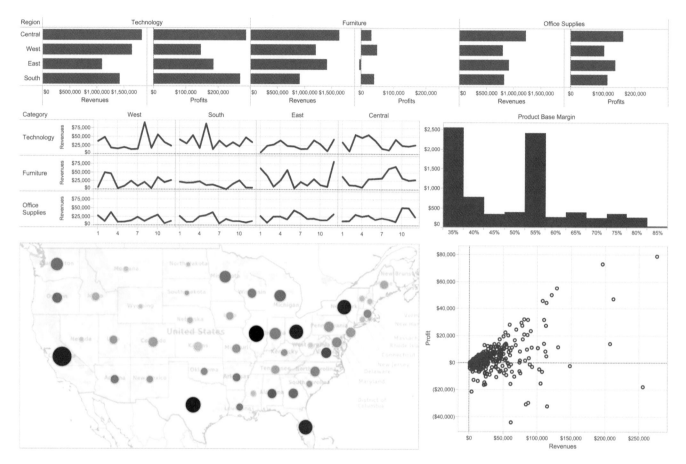

FIGURE 8.12

With more views together in the scene before us, we can detect multivariate relationships that weren't visible when we saw these views individually. For example, notice that during the last month of the year, furniture revenues increased more dramatically in the East than did revenues for other product categories (see the line graph), which might account for furniture's dominance overall in that region (see the upper-left bar graph). But it's possible that the increase was accomplished by offering excessive discounts, resulting in losses (see furniture profits in the East in the upper bar graph). This richer understanding of the whole can become even more full when we interact with the views in a coordinated manner. The perspectives that appear in the five views of revenues and profits above are coordinated not only in the sense that they share a common data set, but also because they are linked such that specific items selected in one view are automatically selected in the others as well. This coordination can affect the data in two potential ways: filtering or highlighting.

Coordinated Filtering

In its present form, the multi-perspective overview of revenues and profits on the previous page can only reveal information at a fairly high level of aggregation. A great deal of variation exists in the data, however, that can only be seen by examining subsets. For example, we can see a peak in the distribution of base product margins in the 35.00-39.99% range and another in the 55.00-59.99% range, but this pattern might not persist in individual product categories. Let's see if the pattern is different for technology products alone. To do this, I've selected "Technology" in the top graph to filter out other product categories in the other graphs (see below).

Not all products support automatic filtering in response to selecting a subset of data (in this case "Technology" in the upper graph). Filtering doesn't have to be initiated in this manner, however. Any convenient means of filtering is fine.

FIGURE 8.13

By looking at the histogram of product base margin, we can see that the peak in the range of 35.00% to 39.99% is not prominent for technology products alone, but the other peak that we previously observed is visible. Connections in other views can be seen as well, such as the fact that profits in California, represented by bubble color intensity on the map, are much lower for technology products than for products overall and that other states with high revenues, such as Texas, do not exhibit lower technology profits. We can also see by glancing at the scatter plot that all six orders with significant losses are associated with technology products.

We could continue to interact with the data, filtering in this coordinated manner to find other multivariate relationships. However, one potential downside of coordinated filtering, which you might have noticed, is that to compare how the data looked before filtering versus after, we must rely on memory, because the "before" version disappears when we filter. For example, we only knew that profits in California were lower for technology products than they were for products overall if we remembered that the bubble was darker before we filtered the data. The next approach—coordinated highlighting—addresses this problem.

Coordinated Highlighting

In contrast to coordinated filtering, coordinated highlighting doesn't remove anything; it simply highlights the selected data. This allows us to focus on the selected data in the midst of and in comparison to the other data. That is, we can focus on a subset of data without losing sight of how that subset relates to the whole. In the example below, we can see the subset of data that was exclusively displayed in the previous example, but this time in a way that allows us to compare it to the entire set and to observe precisely how it differs from the whole.

The technical name for "coordinated filtering" or "coordinated highlighting" is "brushing and linking." "Brushing" is the act of selecting a subset of data in one of the views, just as you might swipe a paintbrush across a selected section of a painting. "Linking" reflects that the views are linked together so that selecting data in one view affects all other views automatically, either by filtering out all other data or highlighting the selected data.

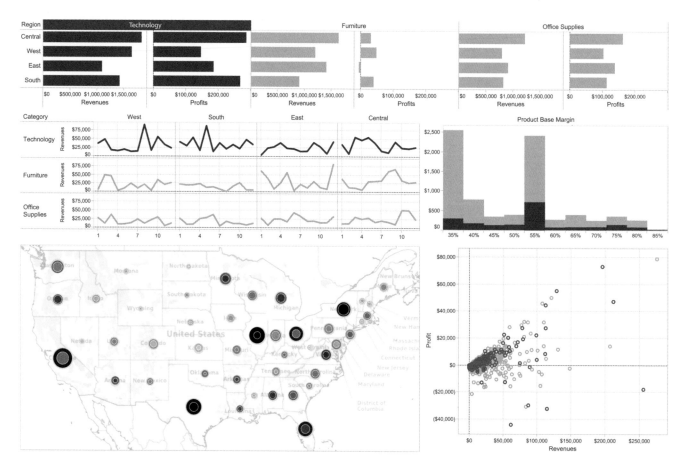

FIGURE 8.14

Now, all of the differences that we would have struggled to see when we were filtering are easy to see. For example, notice in the histogram on the right the minor contribution that technology products make to the prominence of base margins in the 35% to 59% range. Notice in the map that technology sales in California are producing significantly lower profits than sales of other products (the light gray bubble in the center of the much darker bubble). And, finally, notice in the line graphs that the patterns of technology monthly revenues are quite different from the patterns of monthly revenues for furniture and office supplies, which we couldn't see in the filtered view. Examining technology products alone would not reveal any of these insights.

I'm not suggesting that coordinated highlighting is better than coordinated filtering. Not at all. They are both useful for different purposes and lead to different insights. When we only care about a subset of data without needing to compare it to a larger set, filtering works best. When we remove what doesn't interest us from the display, that means we don't need to make an effort to ignore the larger set. Both operations should be readily available, ideally with little more than the click of the mouse to choose between them.

Multivariate Relationships

Some important stories reside in complex relationships among variables. With the exception of our efforts to explore variation within measures, all of our work so far has involved working with more than one variable at once. The kind of multivariate relationships that we'll focus on now involves characterizing things (products, hospitals, regions, etc.) by multiple variables simultaneously to produce a multivariate profile of each, which we will use to find similarities and differences among them.

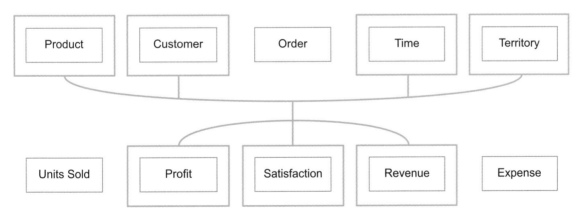

FIGURE 8.15

For example, we might want to see if there is a characteristic multivariate profile that's associated with cars that get the best gas mileage, based on the following variables: class (sedan, couple, SUV, and truck), engine size, weight, year made, and engine type. To do this, we'll rely on a special type of graph called a *parallel coordinates plot*, which was designed for this purpose.

Parallel Coordinates Plots

This graph will allow us to view relationships among many variables—both categorical and quantitative—at once in a single graphical image.

Most graphs have two axes, X and Y, which are arranged perpendicular to one another. Categorical or quantitative scales are labeled along the axes.

Parallel coordinates were first invented by Alfred Inselberg.

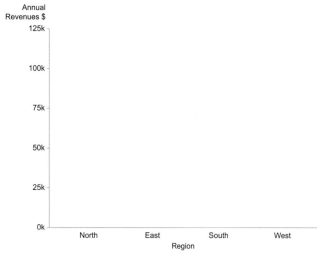

FIGURE 8.16

This form of display, originally developed by the philosopher and mathematician René Descartes, makes quantitative information easy to perceive and interpret, but it's limited to two axes. A third axis, usually called the Z axis, can be added to a graph of this type. However, adding a third axis transforms the graph from a 2-D to a 3-D display, which is no longer easy for our eyes and brains to perceive and interpret. It is useful to be able to position variables along more than two axes; how can this be done without making the graph incomprehensible? One answer is to arrange the axes in parallel to one another rather than perpendicular, as illustrated below.

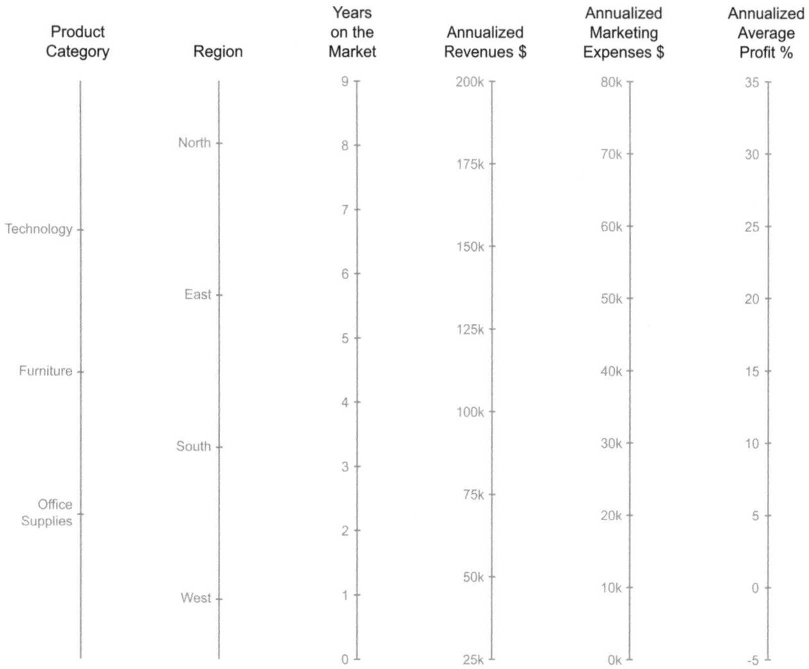

FIGURE 8.17

In this example, we can see six variables that describe products: product category, region, years on the market, annualized revenues, annualized marketing expenses, and annualized average profit percentage. On these axes, I'll now mark the six values that describe a particular product.

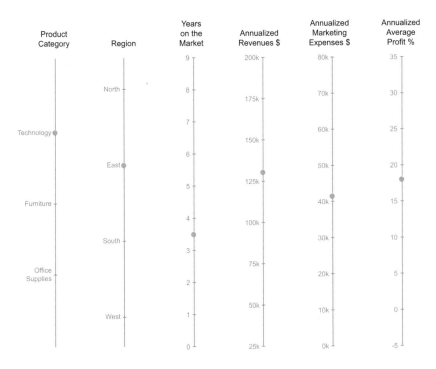

FIGURE 8.18

This product belongs to the technology category. In the East region, it's been on the market for 3 ½ years, has earned approximately $130,000 in annualized revenues, costs roughly $40,000 on an annualized basis to market, and averages about 18% in annualized profit. Now, let's make it easier to see the multivariate attributes of this product as a whole by connecting its attributes and values with a line.

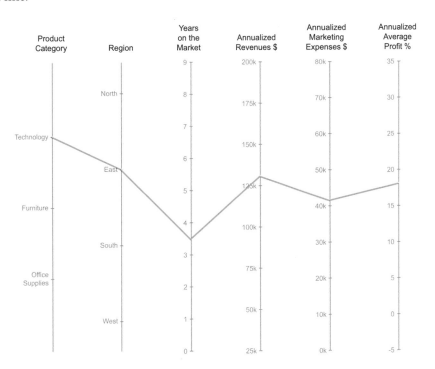

FIGURE 8.19

What we have here is a parallel coordinates plot that displays the multivariate profile of a single product. Now let's plot all 10 of our products for each of the four regions, resulting in 40 lines, color-coded orange for technology, blue for furniture, and green for office supplies.

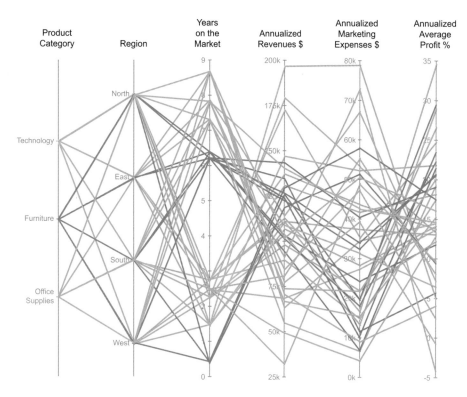

FIGURE 8.20

At first glance, what we have here looks like a cluttered mess, but suspend your disbelief in its potential until I've explained a bit more about it. Even in the midst of this clutter, we can gain a few insights about our products. Here are a few that stand out:

- No technology products have been on the market for more than three years.
- All products have either been on the market for less than three years or for more than six years.
- The four top-grossing items are all technology products.
- The top-grossing item is probably doing well because of a major investment in marketing in a particular region, resulting in a fairly low profit margin.
- The lowest-grossing items are all office supplies.
- The products that have been on the market for the shortest time are all furniture products that earn better than average annualized revenues.
- Four of the top five profit margins are associated with technology products.
- Two office supply products are losing money in particular regions, which in one case appears to be tied to an expensive marketing campaign.

We would also have discovered all of these particular facts when we examined variation within categories. We're not looking at this data in a parallel coordinates plot primarily to remind ourselves of these facts, but to discover complex multivariate relationships that we were not able to examine previously. Because we want to view and compare the multivariate profiles of these products but we can't easily discriminate individual lines in this cluttered display, we'll need to interact with the data in ways that help us focus on particular points of interest.

One of the most common uses of multivariate displays such as this is to see whether items that share a common attribute, such as high profit margins, also share similar profiles within a set of other variables. In the following example, I've selected the four lines with the highest profit margins to highlight them:

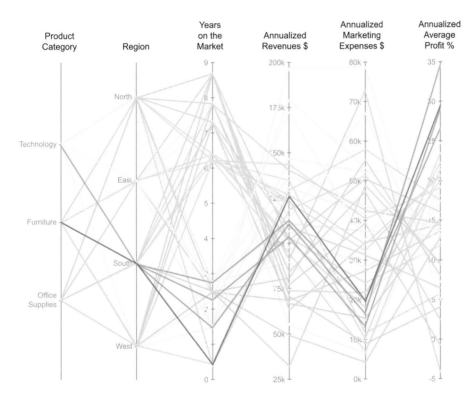

FIGURE 8.21

Now we can see that in all cases the highest profit margins were earned in the South region and were associated with three technology products and one office supply product. All of these products have been on the market for less than three years, all earn annualized revenues within a narrow range from around $21,000 to $25,000, and none were associated with expensive marketing campaigns. The fact that the highest profit margins were all earned in the South region leads us to wonder about sales in the South overall. In the example on the next page, I've filtered out everything except the South (rather than highlighting items sold in the South and leaving the other regions' data visible).

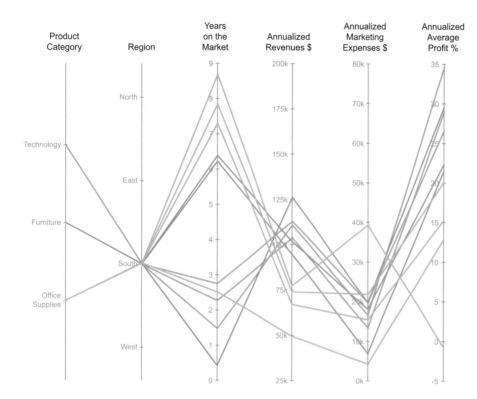

FIGURE 8.22

We can see that revenues in the South are all in the lower half of the range except for one product, and, with few exceptions, the profit margin is high. The one glaring exception to good profits is the office supply product that has been on the market for more than 8 ½ years, which probably lost money because of a marketing campaign that was expensive for this region. In all other cases, marketing expenses were fairly low. One other fact that pops out is that products that have been on the market the longest earn lower revenues in the South than those that have only been on the market for a relatively short time.

This product sales example is simple compared to the much greater level of complexity that we can examine using parallel coordinate plots. We could examine many more than six variables at once, and hundreds of items instead of only forty. We could also interact with the data in a number of additional ways. For example, if we wanted to find multivariate profiles of a particular type, we could instruct the software to search for that multivariate pattern. We could also ask the software to break products into groups based on multivariate similarities using cluster analysis algorithms. What I'm trying to convey here is a sense of what can be done with parallel coordinate plots and the potential they have for extending our understanding of multivariate complexity. Developing this potential takes time, study, and practice.

Having now studied the land from all angles, we've constructed a description that outlines its features. This outline will be the context against which signals will arise, mostly as differences from the norm. We're ready to focus on the task for which we have been preparing during the past eight chapters and on our primary objective as data stewards: detecting signals and taking action in response.

PART II WATCH OVER THE LAND

Now that we're familiar with the land, we're almost prepared take up our duties as stewards watching over it. Almost. We still lack a vision of the land at its best, a record of the land as it is, and the means to monitor the land's well-being at a glance. And, lest we forget the primary purpose of this book, we still need to build the views that will enable us to separate signals from the noise. These are the topics that we'll cover in Part II.

Having surveyed the land of data from every vantage point, we now understand its basic features. We can describe a set of patterns that characterize how it routinely looks and behaves. Most of the signals that we will be looking for will reveal themselves as changes in these patterns. Based on this understanding, we can design and install sensors throughout the land to detect signals. We'll learn to calibrate our sensors to eliminate false alarms while keeping them sensitive enough to prevent signals from slipping by unnoticed. Not all changes in patterns will necessarily matter, so we'll focus on the changes that do. To detect signals, we'll rely on the proven methods of *statistical process control (SPC)*, but we'll apply them in novel ways.

Processes and How They Speak

SPC grew out of the work of Walter Shewhart. He made an important distinction between two types of variation in quantitative information: 1) routine variation—what's expected unless something has changed, and 2) exceptional variation—what's outside the bounds of routine and is therefore a signal. Shewhart created the *control chart* (a.k.a., *process control chart*) to distinguish these two types of variation, which has since become known as a *process behavior chart*.

Donald Wheeler is perhaps the best advocate and teacher of SPC today. His books are excellent, so I won't attempt to duplicate their contents in this book. Instead, I'll briefly introduce SPC to get us started, relying heavily on material from Donald Wheeler's books. In the following paragraphs, Wheeler explains processes and why it's important to distinguish exceptional versus routine variation in them:

> When a process displays predictable variation, that variation may be thought of as the result of many different cause-and-effect relationships where no one cause is dominant over the others. While every process is subject to many different cause-and-effect relationships, predictable processes are those in which the net effect of the multiple causes is a sort of static equilibrium. Deming's terminology for this condition was common cause variation.
>
> On the other hand, when a process displays unpredictable variation, that variation must be thought of as consisting of the sum of the common cause variation plus some additional cause-and-effect relationships. Since the sum is unpredictable, we must conclude that the additional cause-and-effect relationships dominate the common cause variation, and therefore that it will be worth our while to identify these additional cause-and-effect relationships. For this reason Shewhart called these dominant causes assignable causes (also known as special causes).

If we characterize the routine variation of a predictable process as noise, then the exceptional variation of an unpredictable process would be like signals buried within the noise, and a process behavior chart allows us to detect those signals because it filters out the noise.

Donald J. Wheeler (2003). *Making Sense of Data.* SPC Press, page 97.

As you can see, Wheeler's work relates closely to the central theme of this book: detecting signals.

A process is a series of related operations that combine to produce a particular result. Processes express themselves in a language that we can learn.

Before you can improve any system you must listen to the voice of the system (the Voice of the Process). Then you must understand how the inputs affect the outputs of the system. Finally, you must be able to change the inputs (and possibly the system) in order to achieve the desired results... Comparing numbers to specifications will not lead to the improvement of the process. Specifications are the Voice of the Customer, not the Voice of the Process. The specification approach does not reveal any insights into how the process works.

Donald J. Wheeler (2000). *Understanding Variation*, Second Edition. SPC Press, page 21.

What the customer needs is important, but what the customer needs doesn't reveal anything about the process that addresses those needs. To manage a process, we must learn its language and then listen.

Not every time series measures a process. This is important to acknowledge. Most processes can be managed, but this is not true of everything that concerns us. For example, the weather concerns us, but it's mostly beyond our control. Also, let's consider an organization's sales. A sales organization is involved in a *sales process*. The sales process encompasses the aspects of sales that can be managed. We can manage salespeople and how they interact with customers, but we can't manage natural disasters that affect sales in a region. We can't manage—at least until after the fact—shifts in customer sentiment in response to a competitor's product announcement. However, just because we can't control something doesn't mean that we don't care about it. We track and analyze things that are beyond our direct control so that we can do what's possible to make the best of the circumstances. The techniques of SPC are specifically designed to help us maintain and improve effective processes. When we detect signals that are caused by external factors beyond our control—voices other than those of the process—we might not be able to manage those factors, but we might be able to adapt the process to address them.

Wishing Won't Make It So

Wheeler explains that performance targets (e.g., budgets, sales quotas, and service level agreements) are of little use for managing processes. Targets are not derived from the underlying process but are mere, often arbitrary, hopes. A target is a *specification*, not a measure. We cannot use targets to identify abnormal behaviors that signal a change in the underlying process.

The idea of comparing management data to plans, goals, or budgets was transferred directly from the manufacturing practice of comparing product measurements with specification limits. This type of comparison defines the position of the current value relative to some value (possibly arbitrary), with the outcome being a judgment that the current value is either acceptable or unacceptable (either in-spec or out-of-spec). The fact that this approach to the analysis of data will always result in a favorable or an unfavorable outcome will inevitably lead to a binary world view...A natural consequence of this specification approach to the interpretation of management data is the suddenness with which you can change from a state of bliss to a state of torment...Thus, the specification approach to the interpretation of data will inevitably result in periods of benign neglect alternating with periods of intense panic. This on-again, off-again approach is completely antithetical to continual improvement.

Ibid., pages 17-18.

So true, and such a harmful waste. A predictable process will behave as it routinely does until something significant changes. Until then, it is what it is. Berating people for poor performance compared to an arbitrary target is magical thinking, the stuff of fantasy. Setting ambitious goals might be a reasonable activity, but we can't expect these goals to be achieved by doing business as usual. Changes in behavior can only be achieved by changes in the process that are capable of producing the desired state. We must discard our magic wand and examine processes for useful opportunities.

I'm not saying that targets are useless. They're essential if we want to make things better. We just need to be careful that we don't misuse them. When we want to improve a particular performance measure, the first step is to identify a potential change in the process that might produce the desired outcome. Based on our best guess about the possible effects of the change, we can set a realistic target, implement the change, and then monitor the measure to see if and to what extent that change produces the desired outcome. In other words, we must approach the problem scientifically, making hypotheses about the possible effects of particular interventions and then running experiments to see whether our hypotheses have merit. Although we don't always need to control our experiments with the full rigor of the scientific method when we're trying to decrease manufacturing defects or improve profits, we should nonetheless control the variables by introducing and testing one change at a time. Otherwise we won't obtain useful insight into the cause of the outcomes.

Homogeneous Enough for Signal Detection

The more that we aggregate values to higher levels of summary, the more the data transitions from being homogeneous (characterized by sameness) to being heterogeneous (belonging to different groups). For example, when revenues are aggregated to high levels of geography—such as the Europe, Middle East, and Africa region—differences in cultures, languages, economies, governments, and other factors are combined, which all contribute to variation in data. These mergers of routine variation make it difficult to isolate special causes. For this reason, we should track changes in values at a low, relatively homogeneous level, not a highly summarized level.

Later in this chapter, when we look at graphs that are designed to detect signals, we'll find that boundaries between routine and non-routine variation aren't sensitive enough to spot signals if those boundaries are excessively broadened by heterogeneity. Signals can hide out and remain undetected within broad boundaries.

Executive-level reports with highly aggregated data rarely reveal signals. Organizations that attempt to manage performance only at this high level will fail. We must get down into the details where we can track values that are associated with homogeneous processes. Signals identify special causes of behavior. To find them, we must examine data at the level where specific causes exert their influence.

Long and Often Enough for Signal Detection

Along with excessive aggregation, we must face another common enemy of time-series analysis: too little time. If our organization is typical, decisions are often made after comparing a current measure of something to its value at a single point in the past, such as this year compared to last year. This isn't enough time-series information for good decisions. I want to scream when I see performance dashboards filled with trend arrows pointing upward or downward as the only glimpses into history on which managers base decisions. To understand the nature of variation through time, we must, at a minimum, look at a few sequential intervals in time. Wheeler has a firm opinion on this matter:

> *No comparison between two values can be global. A simple comparison between the current figure and some previous value cannot fully capture and convey the behavior of any time series. Yet comparisons of the current value with another value are the most common type of comparisons encountered… While it is simple and easy to compare one number with another number, such comparisons are limited and weak. They are limited because of the amount of data used, and they are weak because both of the numbers are subject to the variation that is inevitably present in real world data. Since both the current value and the earlier value are subject to this variation, it will always be difficult to determine just how much of the difference between the values is due to variation in the numbers, and how much, if any, of the difference is due to real changes in the process.*

Ibid., pages 1, 2, and 5.

> *The traditional limited comparisons, in which a current value is expressed as a percentage of some other value, can neither filter out noise nor highlight potential signals. Large percent differences may be due to noise, and small percent differences may represent signals. Managers who use percent differences exclusively will be misled. They will focus on the wrong items and wonder what went wrong as things get worse.*

Ibid., page 61.

We don't need extensive history to get a sense of what's happening now. For signal detection, ancient history is of little value. What we need are enough time-series values to determine routine behavior. A sequence of at least eight time-series values will usually suffice.

Hand in hand with the question "How many values are sufficient?" we must also ask, "At what interval of time should we measure change?" To answer this question, we must determine the level of frequency at which significant changes in the underlying process occur. In a typical manufacturing process, if manufacturing defects are monitored as a key metric of performance, we usually track defects daily. Tracking them hourly would probably exhibit too much meaningless variation because of events such as scheduled breaks and transitions between outgoing and incoming workers. Tracking defects weekly, however, would hide significant differences in daily behavior that must be managed for us to run the process effectively. When we are monitoring visits to a website, daily tracking might be too fine a level of detail. A website that experiences a great deal of variation in the number of visits on different days of the week, such as fewer visits on weekends, might exhibit a great deal of routine variation from day to day; this routine variation constitutes noise, so weekly measures would be more useful for signal detection. Values that change more slowly, such as those that track global climate change, can't be rushed. In short, we must find the interval of time at which signals occur but aren't hidden in noise.

Signals in Variation through Time

To detect meaningful changes in variation through time, we'll rely on a process behavior chart called an *XmR chart*. It combines two graphs of related time-series values: 1) the *X chart* displays the actual values of a measure as they change through time (e.g., actual daily defects in a manufacturing process), and 2) the *mR chart* ("mR" stands for "moving range") displays the amount of change from one value to the next through that same period of time. Both graphs also display the limits of routine variation. These limits give us historical context for distinguishing routine ("common cause") from exceptional ("special cause") variation. Here's an example of an XmR chart that tracks daily manufacturing defects:

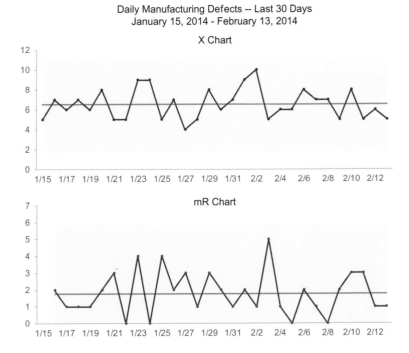

FIGURE 9.1

XmR charts typically display a running series of values consisting of a fixed length of time, such as the past 30 days, past 16 weeks, past 13 months, and so on. The blue line in the previous X chart, called the *central line*, represents the center of routine behavior. It is based on the mean (sometimes the median) of the individual values for a period of time that begins at some point in the past, usually before the first value that appears in the graph itself but after the last significant change in the process. In the previous example, the central line in the X chart represents a mean of 6.5 daily defects. Similarly, the central line in the mR chart represents the mean (sometimes the median) of the moving ranges, called the *average moving range*. In the previous example, the central line in the mR chart represents an average moving range of 1.8, which tells us that, on average, the number of defects changes routinely by 1.8 from day to day. The light-blue shaded areas in both charts mark the limits of routine behavior. The upper and lower limits for the X chart, called the *natural process limits* (a.k.a., three-sigma limits), are calculated by multiplying the average moving range by 2.66 and adding the result to the value of the central line to get the upper limit, or subtracting it from that value to get the lower limit. The upper range limit for the mR chart is calculated as the average moving range multiplied by 3.27. The limits in this example are calculated as follows:

- mR chart upper limit is equal to the average moving range of 1.8, multiplied by 3.27, which is 5.886.
- X chart lower limit is equal to the mean number of defects of 6.5, minus the average moving range of 1.8, multiplied by 2.66, which is 1.712.
- X chart upper limit is equal to the mean number of defects of 6.5, plus the average moving range of 1.8, multiplied by 2.66, which is 11.288.

When a change in the process redefines routine behavior, then the central lines and limits are recalculated, and the shift in routine behavior is reflected in the chart. In the example below, imagine that a new piece of manufacturing equipment was installed effective February 3rd that caused a reduction in defects.

You're probably wondering why we use the scaling factors 2.66 and 3.27 to calculate natural process limits. These factors were developed in SPC to more effectively and usefully set the limits that separate signals from noise. These factors are firmly grounded in mathematics, but the math is a little too complicated to explain in this book. If you're interested, explanations can be found in each of the following books by Donald Wheeler: *Understanding Variation, Twenty Things You Need to Know*, and *Making Sense of Data*.

Daily Manufacturing Defects -- Last 30 Days
January 15, 2014 - February 13, 2014

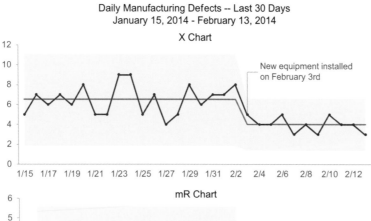

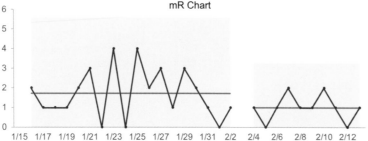

FIGURE 9.2

Beginning on February 4th, the first day on which moving range values could be calculated following the installation of the new equipment, and continuing through February 13th, the average moving range was reduced from 1.7 to 1. In the X chart, based on the daily number of defects beginning on February 3rd and continuing through February 13th, the central line was reduced to 4, and the natural process limits became much tighter. The natural process limit in the mR chart was significantly reduced as well.

Now that we know how the values in an XmR chart are calculated, let's learn to detect signals.

> *Since three-sigma limits will filter out virtually all of the routine variation, any point outside the three-sigma limits is a potential signal. Moreover, the further a point is outside the limits, the stronger the evidence that a change has occurred. False alarms, when they occur, will be rare and will tend to be just barely outside the limits, so as the number of points outside the limits increases, and as their distance outside the limits increases, your confidence will increase that the process is, indeed, being operated in an unpredictable manner.*

Donald J. Wheeler (2009). *Twenty Things You Need to Know.* SPC Press, pages 83-84.

Values that fall outside of the natural process limits are not the only signals; they're just the primary type. Sensitivity to signals can be increased by using a few other rules as well, but here we're going to use only the rules that are most useful and don't require any additions to the XmR chart.

> *Whenever eight successive values on the X Chart all fall on the same side of the central line, you should look for the cause of a small but sustained shift in the underlying process.*

Ibid., page 86.

To review, we'll use XmR charts to identify signals as values that match either of the following two criteria:

Criterion #1: Any value that falls outside the natural process limits

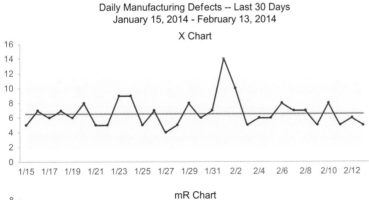

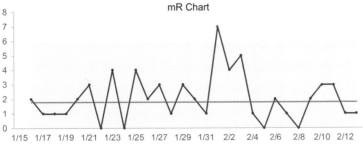

FIGURE 9.3

In this example, values on February 1 in both the X and mR charts fell outside of the natural process limits. This would qualify as a signal even if only one of these two values was located beyond the limits.

Criterion #2: Any eight consecutive values that fall on the same side of the central line

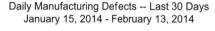

Daily Manufacturing Defects -- Last 30 Days
January 15, 2014 - February 13, 2014

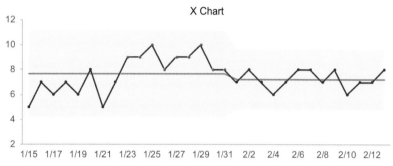

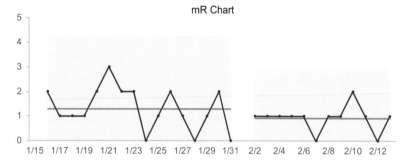

FIGURE 9.4

In the X chart above, I've highlighted as red nine consecutive values located above the central line, which qualify as a signal according to criterion #2. Based on this signal, corrective action was taken to reduce defects, which resulted in a lower central line and tighter limits.

Whenever a change in the process occurs that leads us to recalculate the central lines and natural process limits in an XmR chart, we must be careful to keep in mind that we cannot begin to spot signals following that change until at least eight time-series values have been added. Only then do we have enough data to establish a new basis on which to separate routine from exceptional behavior.

Although these two criteria have the potential to identify values caused by random variation, it is rare for these phenomena to result from randomness. When we see something in an XmR chart that qualifies as a signal based on these criteria, we can feel confident that our efforts to identify the cause will uncover something important.

Remember that in *Chapter 3 – Variation within Measures* we talked about situations when it's not appropriate to use the mean as a measure of a distribution's center. The method that we've been using to calculate the central line in the XmR chart is based on the mean of the average moving range, but on occasion it works better to use the median instead. The centers of distributions that are highly skewed in shape, especially those with a few extreme outliers that influence the mean, can be better described using the median to calculate the *average moving range*. To do this, we calculate the natural process limits a little differently. The scaling factor 2.66 that we usually use to calculate the X chart's limits is replaced with 3.14, and the scaling factor 3.27 that we usually use to calculate the mR chart's limits is replaced with 3.87.

When changes are introduced in a process, and targets are associated with these changes, those targets should appear in the XmR chart. In the following example, the goal is to increase the percentage of times that a weekly email newsletter to customers is opened. Until now, customers only opened the newsletter 15.62% of the time on average, and the routine variation from week to week ranged from 13.52% to 17.72%.

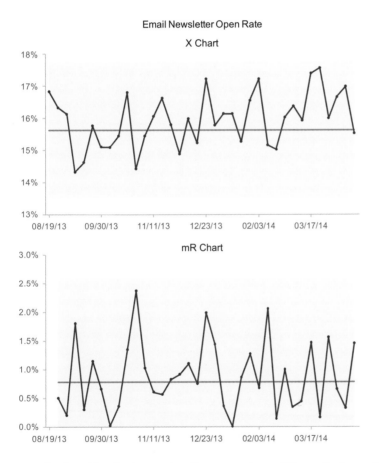

FIGURE 9.5

The company had an idea for increasing the percentage of times that people opened the newsletter and estimated that the average would increase to 17% once the idea was implemented. The blue X that appears eight weeks in the future in the following chart represents this target.

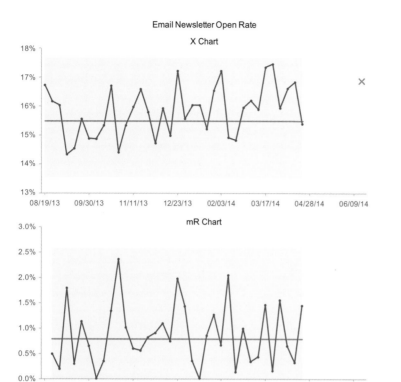

FIGURE 9.6

The company implemented the idea on April 28, 2014 and continued to monitor the measure. They found that, during the next eight weeks, the change produced an improvement that was, in fact, greater than they had estimated. Because the process changed in a way that produced a new average and degree of variability, the central line and limits in the XmR chart were updated to reflect this new norm, as illustrated below.

FIGURE 9.7

Whenever a process changes such that new norms are established, the XmR chart should be updated once enough time-series values have been collected to calculate a new central line and limits. This applies whether the change was intentional or not. The XmR chart allows us to spot both planned and unexpected signals in processes.

I hope it's clear that my introduction to XmR charts in this chapter is brief and somewhat general. What I've touched on, Donald Wheeler covers in great detail with a seasoned veteran's knowledge and experience. XmR charts can enable much more nuanced analysis than we have discussed here, but that requires more training and experience. Let Wheeler be your mentor for that process. I recommend that you begin by reading his book *Understanding Variation*.

Instructions for creating XmR Charts in Excel can be found in Appendix B at the end of this book.

Adaptations of Statistical Process Control

The methods of SPC are typically applied to measures of process performance, but they can also be applied more broadly. These methods can be used to monitor changes to any data pattern that can be described quantitatively. For example, we can describe patterns of variation within categories. We can also describe patterns of variation within measures. In fact, every one of the types of data analysis that we've learned so far in this book involves patterns that we can describe quantitatively. Consequently, we can use XmR charts to look for significant changes in all of the routine patterns of the land that we've observed so far.

Signals in Variation within Categories

We previously considered variation within categories mostly as the degree to which categorical items proportionally contribute to the whole of something (e.g., total revenues by product) and the way that some items stand out as extraordinarily different from the others (i.e., outliers). Not all outliers are signals. We must distinguish what simply is and cannot be altered from what actually matters because we can do something useful about it. For example, a customer who purchases many more products from you than any other customer might just be a customer with a greater purchasing capacity and need than others. This is useful to know, but it isn't a signal if this beneficial behavior cannot be extended to other customers. That is, we can't make our other customers larger to increase their purchasing capacity and needs. The same holds true for outliers that are problems. A hospital with an unusually high post-surgical mortality rate could be the result of circumstances that cannot be controlled, such as the fact that it specializes in only treating the sickest patients. All that we can do is separate the outliers that are eligible for action (the signals) from those that are just part of the landscape.

The primary changes that we look for when considering variation within categories involve the degree to which particular items contribute to the category as a whole. For example, we might look for changes in the degree to which each of our products contributes to the whole of sales, or we might look for changes in incidence of post-surgical infections following a particular procedure among the 10 hospitals in our network.

For purposes of signal detection, we won't need to be concerned with every item in a category, only those that significantly affect our organization's welfare and performance. We'll use the Pareto principle as a rule of thumb to narrow the list of items to the ones that matter. The top items that together contribute up to 80% of the total of critical measures will go on our lists. However, we should not feel bound to follow this principle devoutly. If an item that doesn't belong to the top-80%-contributors' list concerns us for some reason, there's no harm in monitoring it as well.

Imagine that we work for a laptop computer manufacturer, and a category that matters a great deal to us consists of the reasons that customers return computers. Obviously, we would like to reduce the number of returns, so we must understand the reasons and focus on correcting the ones that cause the most returns. In *Chapter 2 – Variation within Categories*, we used the Pareto chart to see the relative contribution of items in a category based on a specific measure. Let's use a Pareto chart now to look at the reasons that customers are returning laptop computers.

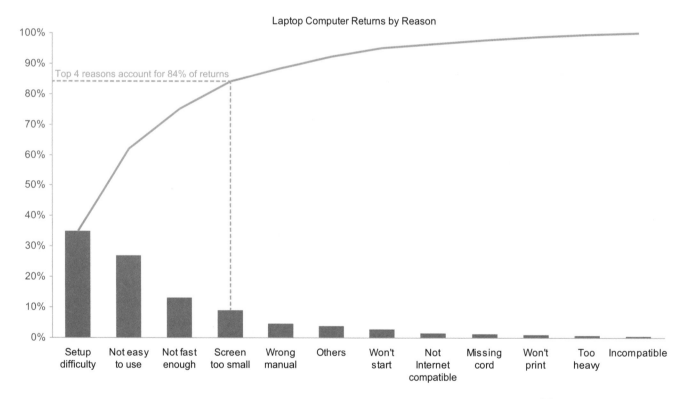

FIGURE 9.8

Let's now narrow the data in the chart to only the reasons associated with approximately 80% of our returns and eliminate the red line of cumulative values.

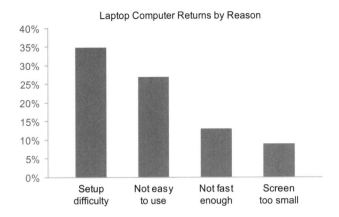

FIGURE 9.9

What we could use now is a version of the graph that monitors changes in this ranked, part-to-whole relationship. Specifically, we want to spot occasions when the magnitude of returns for any of these four top reasons changes significantly. We could use four separate XmR charts, one for each of these reasons, to look for occasions when the actual value of returns matches either of the two criteria that qualify them as signals. This would work, but wouldn't it work even better if we could incorporate these four XmR charts into the graph above in a way that allows us to look for these changes in the context of variation within this category? Indeed it would, so let's do it. Here's an example of how this might look, with the X charts in the plot area of the graph and the mR charts below the X axis:

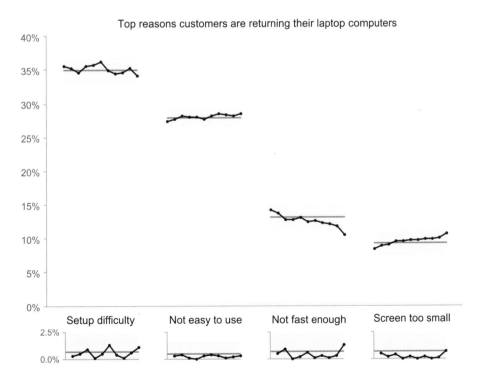

FIGURE 9.10

Now we can see changes in these four reasons for returns. For example, we can see a significant recent reduction in returns due to the laptop computer not being fast enough. Perhaps a celebration is in order. But we can also see that the last eight values for returns due to the screen being too small are above the central line, which is a clear signal of an increasing problem. So much for the celebration.

Signals in Variation within Measures

Imagine that, after months of effort, we managed to improve our manufacturing process, resulting in an acceptable number of routine defects. Based on the last 12 four-week periods (roughly a year), the frequency distribution of daily defects looks like this:

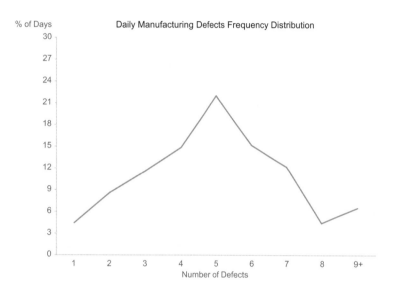

FIGURE 9.11

To detect signals in this distribution, we must periodically check the pattern and compare it to the norm that's been established to make sure that they continue to match. Minor changes will occur that are random and therefore meaningless. To distinguish these from meaningful changes, we must include a range of expected random variation from the pattern. In the example below, the range of routine variation for each daily number of defects, based on roughly a year's worth of prior data, appears as a light-blue rectangle, with a darker blue horizontal line to mark the average.

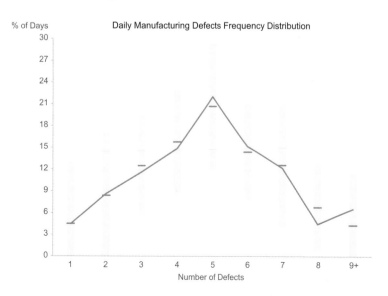

FIGURE 9.12

Where the pattern falls outside of these boundaries, we have a signal, according
to criterion #1. The following graph adds a black line to feature the distribution
of daily defects during the last four-week period.

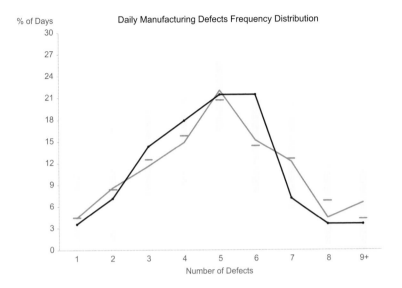

FIGURE 9.13

We can now easily see that during the most recent four-week period the percentage of days on which six defects occurred fell outside of the routine range.
However, this graph doesn't give us a way to spot criterion #2 signals. The
following version solves this problem. The black lines provide individual
time-series values for the last 12 four-week periods.

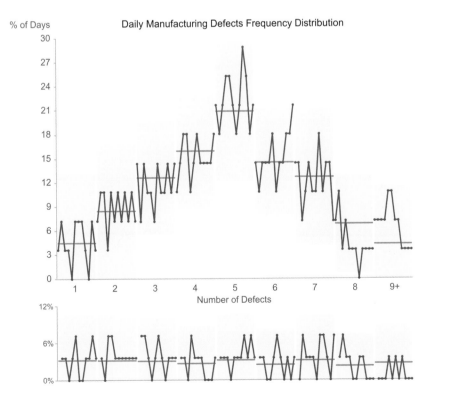

FIGURE 9.14

Now we can see in the X charts that eight daily defects fell below the central
line during the last eight periods and that nine or more daily defects fell above

the central line during the first eight periods of this series, which are both examples of criterion #2 signals. We can also see an example of a criterion #2 signal in the mR charts: two daily defects fell above the central line for the last nine periods.

Even when it isn't necessary to maintain a distribution of particular characteristics, potential signals might still exist. A change in a distribution is not a signal in and of itself, but if that change matters, that is, if something should be done to respond to it, then it is a signal. Take the distribution of people by age in the U.S. This is a case when a distribution of a particular shape isn't necessary, but particular changes in the nature of the distribution might constitute signals. We can think about and discuss what might happen that would constitute a signal with those who best understand the implications of change. For example, the aging population in the U.S. is a signal to healthcare organizations to gear up for increased elder care. It is a signal to the government to make sure that there are funds to cover Social Security payments and increased Medicare costs. If a dip suddenly appears anywhere in the distribution, that would indicate an increase in mortality for a particular age group that might need a response (unless it appears in the youngest age group, which could signal a decline in the birth rate).

Signals in Variation across Space

Spatial signals come in three basic types:

- Values in locations where they didn't previously exist or the absence of values where they did previously exist
- Significant changes in a value's magnitude in a region
- Significant changes in the spatial pattern

All of the ways that we previously learned for spotting changes in spatial values through time can be used to spot these signals.

We must keep in mind that space is an example of a category—an important category for sure, but it's just a category. As such, most of the time we can monitor signals in space as we would look for them in any category. It is only when the location of values in relation to one another is essential to understanding that we must view them on a spatial display, such as a map.

Imagine that we're tracking the number of meals that are being served at each of the eight kitchens that feed the homeless at various locations in the city. We want to monitor changes in the number of meals that are being served at these eight locations in relation to one another to detect the potential movement of people from one to another. To do this, rather than tracking changes in the raw number of meals that are served at each kitchen, we would track changes in proportion by expressing each kitchen's meals as a percentage of the whole. Using XmR charts—one for each kitchen—and positioning them on a map of the city, we could easily detect increases in the proportions of meals being served at one or more kitchens that correspond in time to decreases at one or more nearby kitchens, illustrated on the following page with percentages of meals served for the past 10 weeks.

FIGURE 9.15

Of the eight kitchens, signals of significant change only appear in the two XmR charts in the upper left. In one, the past eight values are below the central line, and in the other these values are above the line. The potential advantage of seeing this on a map is the suggestion, based on the proximity of these two kitchens, that the decrease in activity at the one kitchen might be related to an increase at the other. Perhaps something happened around eight weeks ago that motivated people who were going to the one kitchen to move to the other.

Signals in Relationships among Measures

When we initially examined correlations, the essential nature of each correlation, summarized by fit models, was our focus. Now, signals of two types will surface over time:

- Outliers, which will reveal unusual relationships between variables that might indicate something bad that should concern us or something good that we can put to use
- Changes in the essential nature of correlations, which will alert us to the existence of something new to which we should adjust or that we should seek to use to our advantage

It is relatively easy to detect significant changes in a correlation that is linear because its nature can be described using standard statistics that we can monitor using an XmR chart. The correlation coefficient, slope, and intercept of two quantitative measures—three statistics that all data analysis products provide—sufficiently summarize the nature of a linear correlation. The linear correlation in the scatter plot below is summarized by these three statistics.

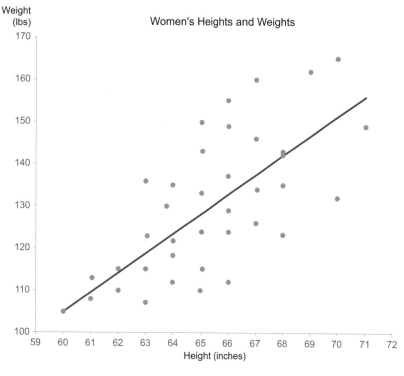

Correlation Coefficient: .707
Slope: 4.64
Intercept: -173.26

FIGURE 9.16

Variation in these statistics could be tracked over a period of time using an XmR chart for each.

When correlations are not linear, changes in their nature cannot be described so easily. We can use fit models to describe a correlation's shape, but no simple statistics characterize that shape. However, we can detect changes in shape using an approach that is similar to the one that we used for distribution relationships. Remember that we can describe the shape of a distribution by dividing its spread into intervals of equal size in a histogram or frequency polygon and determining the routine value and variation for each interval. We can then track changes in these values using XmR charts. Similarly, we can track changes in the shape of a correlation by using XmR charts to monitor the mean of each interval's residuals along the X axis. The scatter plot on the following page shows a non-linear correlation between the hourly utilization rate of equipment in a manufacturing process and the hourly defect rate for 20 days, 16 hours per day, with one value for each hour.

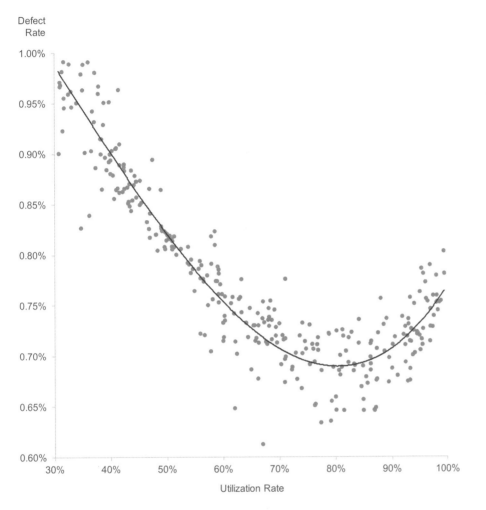

FIGURE 9.17

The greatest rates of defects are associated with low utilization. Defect rates decrease as utilization increases, but at around 80% utilization, the defect rate begins to grow again. The trend line was calculated as a polynomial fit model. This pattern of correlation can be described by dividing the utilization rate into intervals of 10% each and calculating the mean defect rate for each interval, which I've done for the past six months in the table below.

For an explanation of polynomial fit models, see the chapter on correlation analysis in my book *Now You See It.*

Utilization Rate	>=30% & <40%	>=40% & <50%	>=50% & <60%	>=60% & <70%	>=70% & <80%	>=80% & <90%	>=90% & <100%
Mean Defect Rate	0.947%	0.860%	0.786%	0.727%	0.698%	0.692%	0.733%

FIGURE 9.18

Variation in this correlation pattern can be tracked using SPC methods, by calculating the limits of routine variation in defects and, based on this, constructing an XmR chart for each interval along the utilization rate scale. In the following example, the XmR charts each include mean defect rates associated with each utilization interval for the past eleven 20-day periods.

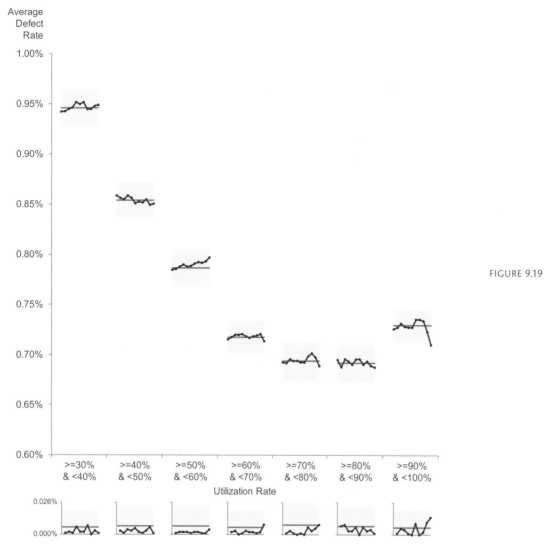

FIGURE 9.19

This arrangement of XmR charts would provide roughly the same information for a non-linear correlation as XmR charts for the slope and intercepts would provide for a linear correlation. However, we still need a way to track changes in the strength of the correlation, which the correlation coefficient gives us for linear correlations. Remember that a linear trend line is drawn through the midst of the data points from left to right in a way that produces the lowest number when the residuals are squared and summed. The correlation coefficient then tells us how well that linear model described the shape of the data. Similarly, we can calculate the residuals in a non-linear correlation, square them to convert all values to positive values, and then sum them to measure the model's ability to describe the correlation—the goodness of the fit. The smaller the sum of the squared residuals, the better the fit. Having determined the mean of the squared residuals over time and its moving average, we can then use a standard XmR chart to track changes in the strength of a correlation. Once again, XmR charts do the job, this time in the context of correlations.

Signals in Relationships among Categories

Just as, when looking for signals in variation within categories, we narrowed the list of categories to those that play significant roles in the organization, we'll do the same when monitoring signals in relationships among categories. For example, if we want to monitor changes in important relationships among our eight sales regions and coffee products based on sales revenues, we would want to monitor all eight regions, but for each we would use the Pareto principle to narrow the list of coffee products to those that produce the greatest revenues. We could then use XmR charts to monitor changes in these sales regions in relation to coffee product inter-category relationships, with a separate chart per region. The chart for a particular region might look like this:

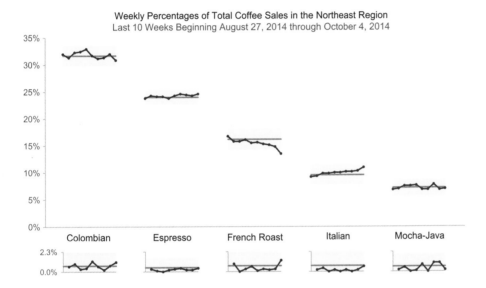

FIGURE 9.20

Bear in mind that the specific products and the number of them that appear in each chart would vary because the number of products that contribute to the top 80% of the revenues would likely vary among regions.

Signals in Multivariate Relationships

Once again, we'll narrow the list of multivariate relationships to those that matter most, and we'll use XmR charts to detect significant changes in these relationships. For this, we'll use the XmR chart to monitor overall changes in the multivariate relationship rather than changes in the individual variables, and we'll display this in the context of a parallel coordinates plot.

Imagine that we work for a large healthcare provider, and we measure the overall healthcare performance of our many hospitals as a composite of the following individual measures:

- Patient satisfaction
- Length of stay
- Post-procedure mortality
- Number of errors
- Number of repeat stays
- Cost of stay

To compare the multivariate profiles of our hospitals, we set the best-performing hospital in each measure to 100% and the worst-performing to 0%, with each other hospital falling somewhere in between. Here's how the multivariate profile of a particular hospital might look when displayed on a parallel coordinates plot:

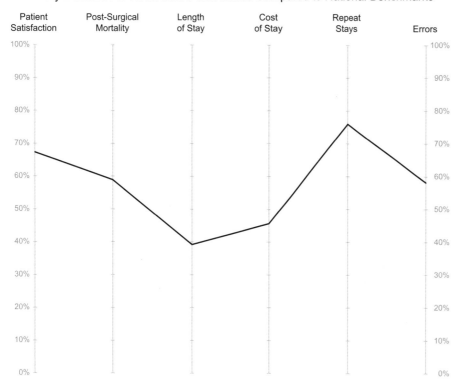

FIGURE 9.21

In a multivariate relationship, the pattern of the overall relationship changes with every change in a single variable that is part of the relationship. There is no single value that I'm aware of that can monitor a change in the overall relationship. We can't aggregate (sum or average) the degree of variation in all of the variables to get a single measure of overall variation because high values in one variable could be cancelled out by low values in others. As a consequence, signals in multivariate relationships must be monitored at the level of the individual variables. It is likely, however, that we're already monitoring signals in these individual variables based on work that we did in the previous section on signals in relationships among categories. If XmR charts have already been built to monitor signals at this level, then all that remains is a way to view these charts together in the context of the multivariate relationship. We can do this by superimposing them on the parallel coordinates plot, illustrated on the following page:

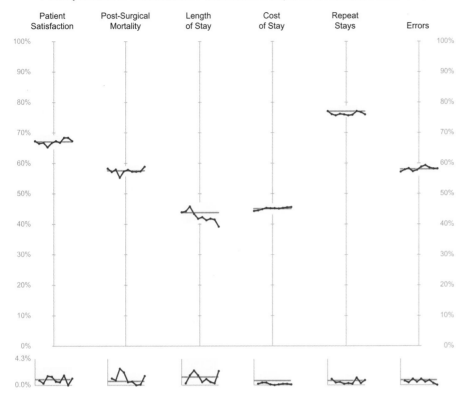

Primary Measures of Healthcare Performance Compared to National Benchmarks

FIGURE 9.22

A signal in any one of the XmR charts would qualify as a signal for the overall multivariate relationship as well.

Sensor Construction

When we were initially exploring the land to get familiar with it, we needed software that offered a great deal of flexibility and an interface that allowed us to move quickly from one view to the next to answer each new question as it arose. However, for ongoing detection of signals that arise in the form of significant changes in patterns over time, we can rely on plain old spreadsheet software, such as Excel. X charts can be easily built in Excel, and each of the charts on which we've superimposed the XmR charts in this chapter can be either created in Excel or displayed in Excel as images. For example, even though Excel doesn't have the native ability to display data on maps, we can easily place a map in Excel as an image and then position XmR charts on the map at specific locations. Even a parallel coordinates plot can be easily constructed for this purpose as a simple line graph if the axes for all variables are standardized to display 0% to 100% scales.

Every display that's needed for ongoing signal detection could be created in a single Excel spreadsheet, such as one organized into a separate worksheet for each type of analysis. In fact, this spreadsheet could serve as the data source for the signal monitoring dashboards that we'll build in *Chapter 12 – Monitor the Land for Signals*. However, I'm not suggesting that we have to use spreadsheet software for signal detection. We can use any tool that provides the means to easily build our XmR charts and update them with fresh data at regular time intervals.

Before beginning to build dashboards for signal detection, there are a few things we should consider as stewards of the land. First, we need to step back and envision the land at its best.

By surveying the land, we've acquired knowledge, but acquiring knowledge isn't our ultimate goal as stewards. Data becomes *information* only when it informs, resulting in understanding. Information becomes *knowledge* when we store it in memory for future reference, either internally in our brains or externally in documents. Knowledge, in turn, is only valuable when we put it to use. So the ultimate goal is not knowledge, but what I call *wisdom*: the act of using what we know to do something good. Thus, decisions and actions that preserve and improve the land are the true goals of our stewardship.

As stewards, we strive to envision the land at its best. We try to preserve ways in which the land is already healthy, watching for signals of deterioration and then working to restore well-being. Preservation is not enough, however. There will always be ways in which the land can be improved. We can be people of vision, imagining the land as better than it already is. This is seldom done, and rarely done well.

The mission statements of organizations do not usually express clear, meaningful vision. Typically, they are little more than marketing platitudes. Here's an example—Volvo's mission statement—of a vision shrouded in fog:

> *By creating value for our customers, we create value for our shareholders. We use our expertise to create transport-related products and services of superior quality, safety and environmental care for demanding customers in selected segments. We work with energy, passion and respect for the individual.*

This is hardly a clear vision that would make employees excited to joyfully greet each new day as they pull in to work at the Volvo factory. Yawn. Actually, what we just read was Volvo's old mission statement. It changed when enough people poked fun at it. Here's Volvo's new mission statement:

> *Our global success will be driven by making life less complicated for people, while strengthening our commitment to safety and the environment.*

It's now shorter, but still mostly marketing-speak, not truly visionary. Most mission statements are written to impress the public, not to provide a clear and honest declaration of the organization's vision to do something of real value for the world.

This isn't a book about mission statements, and as stewards—people who work with data to understand, preserve, and improve organizations—we might not have much input, if any, into mission statements that appear on the "About" page of our organization's website. We can, however, use our evidence-based knowledge of the organization to imagine meaningful goals.

Unlike mission statements, which may be abstract expressions of vision, an organization's goals must be tangible. Greenpeace is an environmental organization that I've supported for many years. (Yes, I'm a tree-hugger.) The organization's mission statement clearly states what it does:

> *We defend the natural world and promote peace by investigating, exposing and confronting environmental abuse, and championing environmentally responsible solutions.*

Here, in a nutshell, we have a description of Greenpeace that's appropriately abstract to cover the breadth of its work but also clear. It captures the essence of the Greenpeace's purpose. Love them or hate them, this is who they are and what they do. If we worked for Greenpeace as stewards of the land, we would rely on data to determine how well its work of "investigating, exposing and confronting environmental abuse, and championing environmentally responsible solutions" is succeeding. We would monitor the world for signals of new environmental abuses and opportunities. Goals can sometimes only be achieved through unprecedented approaches that require extraordinary imagination and effort, and are only worthwhile if they are translated into realistic plans to get from where we are to where we want to be. Goals can and should force us to extend our reach, but not in ways that require superhero abilities. For us to be able to pursue them, goals must also be concrete, by which I mean well defined and measurable. A goal is worthless if we have no way to determine whether we've attained it.

Goals are only worthwhile if they help us achieve things that matter. What matters? Something that restores, preserves, or improves well-being, however we define well-being for ourselves or for those whom we support. If we believe that maximizing shareholders' earnings is what matters most, that's our right, but, in and of itself, this isn't a goal that will produce ongoing, worthwhile results. It's too narrow-minded and selfish. To produce a profitable venture, we must provide something worthwhile to more than just our shareholders. Worthwhile goals distribute well-being more broadly than just to our investors.

One of the dangers of overly narrow, selfish goals that focus exclusively on the well-being of the few is that these goals tend to be nearsighted. Many corporations can't think past their next quarterly results. Only goals that look further into the future—much further—can sustain an organization's efforts. Short-term goals are fine when they serve as well-placed stepping stones to larger, longer-term goals.

Many goals are established to feed the egos of executives without consideration for the effect of these goals on others. The employees who must live with, strive for, and be judged according to such goals don't find them inspiring, and why should they? Self-aggrandizing goals of executives are not rooted in anything that matters to the organization, nor are they derived from realistic assessments of what's possible. They're nothing more than prods to goad the workers into action to serve the executive's interests while he or she stands on a pedestal of power and shouts orders. Goals of this type incite fear and resentment, not inspiration and loyalty. "You will increase revenues by 10% each quarter (or else)!" "You will deliver this project in three months (or there's the door)!" Many of us have, at some point in our careers, found ourselves in a room surrounded by co-workers as the CEO pumps his fist and leads the cheer "We're number one! We're number one!" If you're like me, you were embarrassed or offended by the scene and looked for a way to slip out unnoticed. We're adults. Inspiration doesn't need to be manipulated; it will arise naturally from within when we encounter a meaningful vision that's aligned with our values.

Enlivened by clear visions of what a land can become, we don't set goals to realize these visions without first finding a path to get us from where we are to where we want to be. We find that path by studying the data: evidence of what is and what can be. What concrete steps can we take to get us there? What changes to the process will align us with that direction? Our data-based insights must be combined with the experience-based insights of others to construct this path. Merely wishing to get there, no matter how vigorously and convincingly the CEO shouts, won't make it happen. Getting there requires knowledge and intelligence. This is the stuff of which worthwhile goals are formed and the way that they are eventually attained.

Our data is a primary source of the knowledge from which we can use our intelligence to formulate achievable, inspirational goals. The better we understand relationships in the data—especially causal relationships—the better we're equipped to identify steps that can be taken to achieve our goals. If we base our goals on evidence of what's possible rather than mere wishes, we'll have a real chance of reaching them.

11 DOCUMENT THE LAND

We've approached each type of variation within and relationship between variables in roughly the same manner: first, by becoming familiar with the norms; next, by identifying what's unusual and making sense of it; and, finally, by identifying ways to spot signals. What's "normal" in this context has nothing necessarily to do with what's right or desirable, or with an organization's goals. What's normal is simply what usually is. Good or bad, it is how things ordinarily behave. Outliers, to the contrary, are what sometimes occur beyond the realm of normality for three possible reasons: 1) random variation, which we learn to ignore; 2) error, which we strive to correct; and 3) unusual circumstances, which we seek to understand, and if possible, coax into the realm of control. Advantageous outliers invite us to embrace new opportunities; harmful outliers incite us to do battle. Norms and outliers combine to form context—a foundation of understanding—based on which we can detect, come to understand, and then respond to signals.

In this chapter, we'll document this context by recording what we've learned. We'll do this to solidify the context in our minds, to plan how we'll use it, and to confirm that the land has been fully surveyed. Documenting the land is a checklist-type process to make sure that nothing important has been is left out.

Externalize the Model

Unless we're savants with extraordinary memory, we can't carry everything we've learned about the land in our heads for easy and immediate recall. We must document our findings in a way that is readily accessible and clear. In other words, because we can't hold all of the information in our heads, we need an external form of storage (a printed or electronic record) to augment our memories. Imagine a binder or an electronic document filled with a well-organized summary that we can immediately access whenever needed.

We'll organize our records primarily around specific measures and categories. Each entry will feature observations about the following:

1. Norms
2. Outliers (measures only)
3. Signals

In the "norms" section for each measure, we'll include subsections for documenting the norms associated with each of the following:

- Variation within categories
- Variation within measures
- Variation through time
- Variation across space
- Relationships between measures

In the "norms" section for each category, we'll include subsections for documenting the norms associated with each of the following:

- Variation within categories
- Relationships among categories
- Variation in multivariate relationships

What I'm proposing in this chapter isn't rocket science. It's just plain old common sense of the type that is less common than it ought to be.

We can document our records using any number of software products, from something as simple as a word processing program (e.g., Microsoft Word) or a set of hyperlinked web pages, to something as sophisticated as a database application that has been customized for the task. Whatever we choose, it must enable easy data entry, integration, and organization of text and graphs.

Sample Documentation

Let's consider the kind of information that we'll record and the way it should be organized, using a measure named "Website Visitor Count" as an example. In the example that begins on the next page, I've included placeholders as comments in brackets for text and graphs that we would include in an actual set of documentation.

Website Visitor Count

Associated Categories:

- Visitor ID
- Visitor Type
- Web Page

Norms:

VARIATION WITHIN CATEGORIES

Web Page

[Insert ranked bar graph.]

[Describe the variation and its meaning.]

Visitor Type

[Insert ranked bar graph.]

[Describe the variation and its meaning.]

VARIATION WITHIN MEASURES

Overall

[Insert frequency polygon.]

[Describe the variation and its meaning.]

Per Location

[Insert frequency polygon.]

[Describe the variation and its meaning.]

Per Page

[Insert frequency polygon.]

[Describe the variation and its meaning.]

VARIATION THROUGH TIME

Overall

[Insert line graph per month.]

[Describe the variation and its meaning.]

[Insert line graph per day for last 30 days.]

[Describe the variation and its meaning.]

[Insert cycle plot per day for last three months.]

[Describe the variation and its meaning.]

Per Location

[Insert line graph per month.]

[Describe the variation and its meaning.]

Per Page

[Insert line graph per month.]

[Describe the variation and its meaning.]

VARIATION ACROSS SPACE

Visitor Location

[Insert map.]

[Describe the variation and its meaning.]

RELATIONSHIPS AMONG MEASURES

Order Count

[Insert scatter plot.]

[Describe the variation and its meaning.]

Revenue

[Insert scatter plot.]

[Describe the variation and its meaning.]

Outliers:

- Holidays are typically low.
- Election days are typically low.
- Marketing campaigns often produce temporary peaks.
- System outages produce low values.

Signals:

1. Any daily value beyond the natural process limits
2. Any eight consecutive daily values that are either all above or all below the central line
3. Any daily value that is beyond the natural process limits on the cycle plot
4. Any reduction of 20% or more in the strength of the correlation with Revenue, based on the correlation coefficient

––––––––––––

The information that we record about measures includes a fair amount of information about related categories as well, but it's also useful to record information about important categories separately to organize the relevant facts for easy lookup. Let's look at an example that features a category named "Product Family."

Product Family

Item Count: 7

Hierarchical Relationship:

1. Product Line
2. **Product Family**
3. Product
4. Product Version

Associated Measures:

- Units Sold Count
- Revenue
- Expense
- Profit

Norms:

VARIATION WITHIN CATEGORIES

Units Sold Count
[Insert ranked bar graph.]
[Description of the variation and its meaning.]

Revenue
[Insert ranked bar graph.]
[Describe the variation and its meaning.]

Expense
[Insert ranked bar graph.]
[Describe the variation and its meaning.]

Profit
[Insert ranked bar graph.]
[Describe the variation and its meaning.]

RELATIONSHIPS AMONG CATEGORIES

Sales Territory, mediated by Revenue
[Insert a crosstab of bar graphs.]
[Describe the variation and its meaning.]

Customer Type, mediated by Revenue
[Insert a crosstab of bar graphs.]
[Describe the variation and its meaning.]

Customer Type, mediated by Profit
[Insert a crosstab of bar graphs with coordinated highlighting to feature
one or two Product Families in particular.]
[Describe the variation and its meaning.]

MULTIVARIATE RELATIONSHIPS

Region, Customer Type, Units Sold Count, Revenue, Expense, Profit
[Insert a parallel coordinates plot.]
[Describe the variation and its meaning.]

Signals:

1. Any change in rank greater than two levels in a month, mediated by Units Sold Count
2. Any change in rank greater than two levels in a month, mediated by Revenue
3. Any change in rank greater than two levels in a month, mediated by Expense
4. Any change in rank greater than two levels in a month, mediated by Profit

---

The purpose of these examples is not to provide a rigid template for documentation, but instead to suggest the types of information that this documentation should include and a useful way that it can be organized. The actual form that this documentation takes is adaptable to our specific needs.

As stewards, we aren't necessarily among those who manage our organization's performance. It is our job, however, to make sure that the folks who are responsible have convenient ways to monitor what's going on, including signals of significant change. These folks usually juggle full plates of diverse activities. They live close to the action. They might be analytically minded, but they are rarely data analysts, and they don't usually spend much time examining the data themselves. Making it easy for them to maintain an overview of current activity and to anticipate the near future is our responsibility. We can do this, in part, by building performance monitoring dashboards for these folks to use.

Do we as stewards need dashboards to do our own work? Even though I've written a book and teach courses about dashboard design, in my opinion the answer is "Probably not." A dashboard, as I define it, is an information display that enables someone to rapidly monitor what's going on. As such, it's ideal for those whose roles in the organization allow little time for poring over data but require an immediate response when something needs attention. In contrast, as stewards, we live in the data. We can spend hours a day exploring data and examining reports to view the land in ways that others cannot. We don't necessarily need a summarized information display to support quick action; we spend our time investigating the details and then designing such displays for others who don't have time or inclination to explore as we do. Those who manage performance typically focus on a defined set of metrics that inform their work. We, on the other hand, spend our days watching over the land as a whole, which can involve hundred of variables. A dashboard for rapidly monitoring hundreds of variables in a meaningful way is not possible or necessary.

To track signals among the broad assortment of variables that concern us as stewards, it usually works best to maintain a collection of reports filled with XmR charts along with complementary tables and graphs, organized by subject area. Those who are responsible for responding to the signals aren't always able to identify and understand the causes of those signals, especially when data analysis is required. The subject area expertise of those who respond to signals must often partner with our analytical expertise and comprehensive overview of the data. We needn't wait for them to ask for our help. Sometimes our perspective will make us aware of problems and opportunities that others will miss.

The typical person responsible for responding to signals manages a specific function in the organization. A regional sales manager, a manufacturing supervisor, a hospital administrator, a high school teacher, and a military platoon leader are all examples of people who have a specific sphere of responsibility that requires ongoing vigilance and timely response to signals. They could all benefit from well-designed dashboards that rapidly update their situational awareness. A dashboard should provide a single, consolidated overview of the information that requires their attention, with signals highlighted in a way that pops out visually. Further information related to those signals should be easily and immediately accessible from the dashboard in pop-up windows or separate screens.

Imagine a dashboard that could be used by someone in charge of monitoring the performance of a public bus system. The metrics in this case are the following ("KPI" stands for "key performance indicator"):

Category	Metric	Historical Context
KPIs	Buses Running Late Count During the Last Hour	Last 14 days for this day and hour
	Buses Running Late Yesterday > 10% of Stops	Last 14 days
	Drivers Absent Percentage Now	Daily, last 14 including today
	Rider Count Yesterday	Daily, last 8 weeks for this particular day of the week
	Buses Out of Service Count Now	Aging data consisting of 1, 2, 34, 5-7, 8-10, 11-14, and > 14 days
Incidents & Complaints	Collision and Traffic Violations Count Today	Last 8 weeks
	Vandalism Count Today	Last 8 weeks
	Other Crimes Count Today	Last 8 weeks
	Illnesses and Injuries Count Today	Last 8 weeks
	Complaint Count Today	Last 8 weeks
	Other Incidents Count Today	Last 8 weeks

A dashboard could be designed to display these metrics with XmR charts for each. The following example illustrates one way in which this dashboard could be designed:

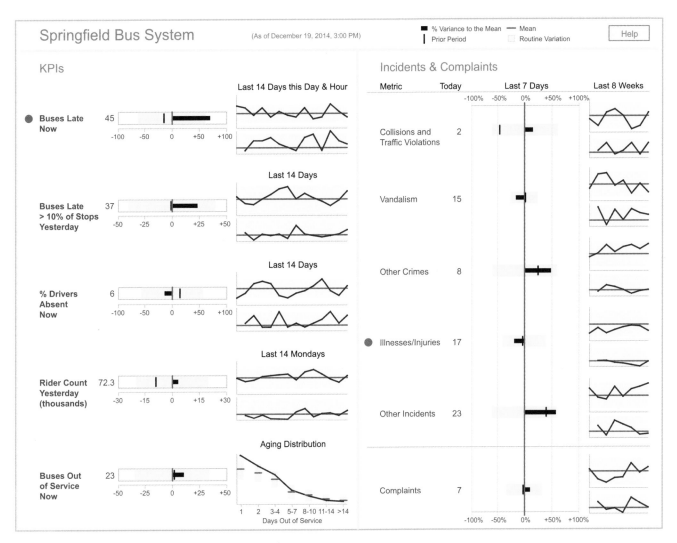

FIGURE 12.1

In this example, situations that potentially require an immediate response have been highlighted by the red alert icons that appear next to the associated metrics. This would allow the user to spot situations of concern immediately, without having to first read the XmR charts. The XmR charts provide the context that is necessary to see the nature of the change that's triggered the alert icons. These alerts do not imply "Look only at these metrics," but "Look at these metrics immediately." All of the data that appears on the dashboard is required to maintain situation awareness, even when all is well.

Take care to keep performance monitoring dashboards focused on the metrics that not only matter but also require rapid response when signals arise. Signals that matter, but don't necessarily need to be constantly monitored in a way that supports an immediate response, can be tracked using other forms of reports that aren't designed for rapid scanning.

As stewards, we can develop dashboards and reports to be used by those who are responsible for managing performance. We need to train these folks in the

For instruction in dashboard design, see my book *Information Dashboard Design*, which covers this topic thoroughly.

use of these dashboards and reports, which requires a basic understanding of SPC and XmR charts. Without an understanding of the ways in which values vary through time—the difference between routine versus special cause variation—these folks might be inclined to knee-jerk reactions to routine variation. Nothing that we do will make a difference if the people responsible for the organization's performance don't understand its causal nature. We can't hide in the shadows, working anonymously in the dim light of our computer screens. As stewards, we must work with people as teachers and advisers.

EPILOGUE – ZEN STEWARDSHIP

As I see it, data stewardship is more than a job. It is perhaps because of my early experience as a minister that I think of it as a "calling." We have an opportunity to enrich our organizations and the lives of our co-workers by helping them base decisions on real evidence of what's happening in the world. When we base our knowledge of the world on evidence and then base our decisions on that knowledge, we usually make better decisions. It is because of this that I love the work that we do. We get to help people make better decisions that can potentially lead to a better world. This is a privilege: one that I genuinely cherish and never take lightly.

Our world is full of noise and it's getting noisier every day. In his song "Signal to Noise," Peter Gabriel sings these words:

> *And in this place, can you reassure me*
> *With a touch, a smile – while the cradle's burning*
> *All the while the world is turning to noise*
> *Oh the more that it's surrounding us*
> *The more that it destroys*
> *Turn up the signal*
> *Wipe out the noise*

He sings these words with great feeling. After the refrain, "Send out the signals deep and loud," Gabriel sings on.

> *Man, I'm losing sound and sight*
> *Of all those who can tell me wrong from right*
> *When all things beautiful and bright*
> *Sink in the night*
> *Yet there's still something in my heart*
> *That can find a way*
> *To make a start*
> *Turn up the signal*
> *Wipe out the noise*
>
> *Wipe out the noise*
> *Receive and transmit*
> *Receive and transmit*
> *Receive and transmit*

As stewards of the land, it is our job to "receive and transmit." We are conduits of enlightenment. I make no apologies for presenting our work as an important mission.

I once ended a keynote presentation at a large technical conference by playing John Lennon's song "Imagine," accompanied by a series of images.

> *Imagine no possessions*
> *I wonder if you can*
> *No need for greed or hunger*
> *A brotherhood of man*
> *Imagine all the people*
> *Sharing all the world...*
>
> *You may say I'm a dreamer*
> *But I'm not the only one*
> *I hope someday you'll join us*
> *And the world will live as one*

A few days later, someone wrote a public statement criticizing my use of the song as offensively inappropriate for a technical conference. This caught me off-guard. Inappropriate? Offensive? The motives that energize and guide my personal life are no less active in my professional life. By drawing a firm line between their personal and professional lives, people often behave badly—immorally—and justify their actions as "just doing business." Pharmaceutical companies sometimes promote drugs that they know are ineffective. They might have conducted 20 clinical trials, the first 19 of which indicated that the drug had no efficacy, but when the 20th, through random chance, suggested a slight benefit, that's the only study that they made public. Banks make risky loans to people who don't understand the risk, masking the threat in piles of intentionally obscure documentation. When the inevitable happened in 2007 and people lost their homes, the banks were bailed out and are now gradually reintroducing some of the same risks. The list of bad behaviors is long. We are what we do, including what we do at work. There is no excuse for bad behavior in any aspect of our lives.

In this book, we've learned how to survey the land, becoming intimately familiar with its terrain. We do this because we care. We've learned how to discriminate signals from the noise. We've learned how to apply XmR charts in various ways to monitor the land for signals. We're prepared to sound the alert when necessary to preserve and improve the land. Our relationship to the land, however, has only begun. Our ability to serve as good stewards has also just begun.

This book is but a beginning, an introduction. I titled this epilogue "Zen Stewardship" for a reason. In 1970, Shunryu Suzuki, a great teacher of Zen, opened his book *Zen Mind, Beginner's Mind* (1970) with the following words: "In the beginner's mind there are many possibilities, but in the expert's there are few." No matter how much we learn and how expert we become, we do well if we persist in seeing ourselves as beginners. If I've become a good teacher over the years, it is because I've always seen myself primarily as a student with a vast ocean of learning ahead of me. As I face this opportunity, I know that I know very little. I don't find this discouraging, but exciting. I don't find this limiting, but expansive. Only the belief that we've *become* can keep us from *becoming*.

Please use what you've learned in this book as one in a series of stepping stones to ever-growing skill in data sensemaking. If you do, you will help to usher in an "information age" worthy of the name.

Steve

Appendix A   CREATING QUANTILE PLOTS IN EXCEL

Even though Excel does not include a quantile plot as a specific chart, it can be used to create one without great difficulty. Here's quantile plot that I created in Excel:

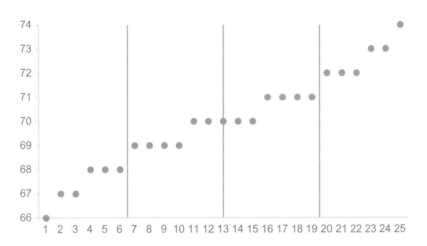

FIGURE A.1

The technique that I used to produce this example was provided by my friend and colleague Jon Peltier of www.peltiertech.com.

Getting the values to display in the graph as dots is the easy part. First, we place the values in one column and the ranked values (1, 2, 3,...) that will appear along the X axis in another column (illustrated below).

Rank	Value
1	66
2	67
3	67
4	68
5	68
6	68
7	69
8	69
9	69
10	69
11	70
12	70
13	70
14	70
15	70
16	71
17	71
18	71
19	71
20	72
21	72
22	72
23	73
24	73
25	74

FIGURE A.2

We use a line graph with dots along the line to display the values, but turn the line off, leaving only the dots.

Now, for the harder part: the vertical lines that mark quartile 1, the median, and quartile 3. This requires a bit of trickery. First, we must calculate the following values:

- Minimum value in the data set
- Maximum value in the data set
- Quartile 1 of the ranked values
- Median of the ranked values
- Quartile 3 of the ranked values

Here is how I usually arrange these values:

Min & Max Values	66	74
Quartile 1	6.5	6.5
Median	13	13
Quartile 3	19.5	19.5

We can use Excel's "MIN," "MAX," and "PERCENTILE.EXC" formulas to calculate these. Notice that we enter the percentiles and median twice, side-by-side, because the technique that we'll use to create the lines requires this redundancy.

Next, we create the line for quartile 1. To do this, we add a new data series to the graph and set "Quartile 1" as its name, the "Min & Max Values" as its Y values, and the two quartile 1 values as its Category (x) axis labels. The result looks like this:

In this example, the values that are used to create the quartile 1 line currently appear as two black dots. These values may appear as a different shape and color when you create the graph, but it doesn't matter because the dots will soon disappear.

Next, we change the chart type of the new quartile 1 data series from a line graph to Straight Lined Scatter plot (i.e., one with a straight line and no dots), which results in the following:

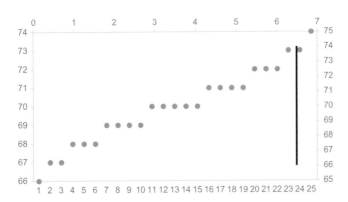

FIGURE A.6

What will soon serve as our quartile 1 line now appears as a black vertical line in this example.

Next, we switch the quartile 1 data series from the secondary axis, which Excel assigned it to automatically, to the primary axis. We do this by 1) selecting the line, 2) accessing the formatting menu, 3) selecting Format Data Series, 4) selecting Axis, and finally 5) selecting Primary Series. The result looks like this:

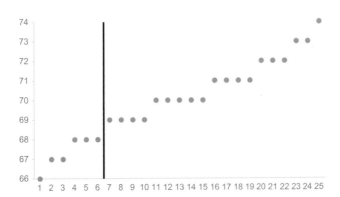

FIGURE A.7

Now that the line appears in the correct location along the X axis, we can format it to appear as we like. In the example below, it has been formatted to appear as a thin, light gray line.

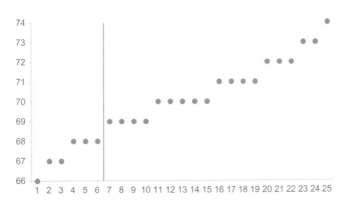

FIGURE A.8

To complete the graph, we repeat the previous steps to create the median and quartile 3 lines, resulting in the following finished quantile plot:

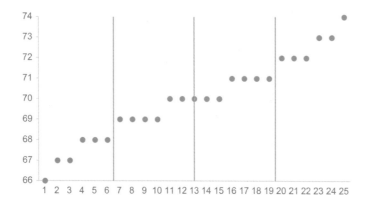

FIGURE A.9

If this seems like a lot of work, we can all take comfort in the fact that a template can be set up to do most of this work for us. This is precisely what I've done. You can download a copy at:

www.perceptualedge.com/signal/quantile_plot_template.xlsx

To create an XmR chart in Excel, begin by downloading a copy of my XmR Chart Template for Excel at www.perceptualedge.com/signal/xmr_template.xlsx This Excel file contains three worksheets, the first of which is the template. The other two worksheets contain XmR chart examples to illustrate the existence of a target and the existence of a change in the process resulting in new calculations for the central line and natural process limits.

Date	Measure	Central Line	Moving Ranges	Average Moving Range	Limits Upper Range Limit	Limits Lower Natural Process Limit	Limits Upper Natural Process Limit	Lower Natural Process Limit Target	Target Central Line Target	Upper Natural Process Limit Target
01/01/09	810.00	4,108.00				-30,984.46	39,200.46			
02/01/09	12,175.00	4,108.00	11,365.00	13,192.65	43,139.98	-30,984.46	39,200.46			
03/01/09	692.00	4,108.00	11,483.00	13,192.65	43,139.98	-30,984.46	39,200.46			
04/01/09	-4,507.00	4,108.00	5,199.00	13,192.65	43,139.98	-30,984.46	39,200.46			
05/01/09	-9,062.00	4,108.00	4,555.00	13,192.65	43,139.98	-30,984.46	39,200.46			
06/01/09	-7,022.00	4,108.00	2,040.00	13,192.65	43,139.98	-30,984.46	39,200.46			
07/01/09	-9,570.00	4,108.00	2,548.00	13,192.65	43,139.98	-30,984.46	39,200.46			
08/01/09	-11,308.00	4,108.00	1,738.00	13,192.65	43,139.98	-30,984.46	39,200.46			
09/01/09	19,710.00	4,108.00	31,018.00	13,192.65	43,139.98	-30,984.46	39,200.46			
10/01/09	19,140.00	4,108.00	570.00	13,192.65	43,139.98	-30,984.46	39,200.46			
11/01/09	11,000.00	4,108.00	8,140.00	13,192.65	43,139.98	-30,984.46	39,200.46			
12/01/09	-11,759.00	4,108.00	22,759.00	13,192.65	43,139.98	-30,984.46	39,200.46			
01/01/10	-11,810.00	4,108.00	51.00	13,192.65	43,139.98	-30,984.46	39,200.46			
02/01/10	24,842.00	4,108.00	36,652.00	13,192.65	43,139.98	-30,984.46	39,200.46			
03/01/10	19,878.00	4,108.00	4,964.00	13,192.65	43,139.98	-30,984.46	39,200.46			
04/01/10	2,297.00	4,108.00	17,581.00	13,192.65	43,139.98	-30,984.46	39,200.46			
05/01/10	-11,292.00	4,108.00	13,589.00	13,192.65	43,139.98	-30,984.46	39,200.46			
06/01/10	3,809.00	4,108.00	15,101.00	13,192.65	43,139.98	-30,984.46	39,200.46			
07/01/10	10,581.00	4,108.00	6,772.00	13,192.65	43,139.98	-30,984.46	39,200.46			
08/01/10	15,046.00	4,108.00	4,465.00	13,192.65	43,139.98	-30,984.46	39,200.46			
09/01/10	54,084.00	4,108.00	39,038.00	13,192.65	43,139.98	-30,984.46	39,200.46			
10/01/10	-9,735.00	4,108.00	63,819.00	13,192.65	43,139.98	-30,984.46	39,200.46			
11/01/10	-5,537.00	4,108.00	4,198.00	13,192.65	43,139.98	-30,984.46	39,200.46			
12/01/10	-7,958.00	4,108.00	2,421.00	13,192.65	43,139.98	-30,984.46	39,200.46			
01/01/11	13,225.00	4,108.00	21,183.00	13,192.65	43,139.98	-30,984.46	39,200.46			
02/01/11	1,722.00	4,108.00	11,503.00	13,192.65	43,139.98	-30,984.46	39,200.46			
03/01/11	1,465.00	4,108.00	257.00	13,192.65	43,139.98	-30,984.46	39,200.46			

FIGURE B.1

This template is a revised version of one that was created by Stacey Barr, the Performance Measure Specialist and author of *Practical Performance Measurement*. Stacey is an expert in the use of XmR charts for performance management. You can learn more about Stacey's work at www.staceybarr.com.

Particular cells are lightly shaded to indicate that they require data entry. Cells that are not shaded do not ordinarily require data entry because they contain Excel formulas for automatically populating the data based on the data that is entered.

Here's an explanation of the columns and how they're used:

- *Date*: For entering the dates for which data will be displayed. The template includes sample dates in the form of months, but any dates can be entered.
- *Measure*: For entering the quantitative values.
- *Central Line*: For the average of the quantitative values. The shaded cell contains a formula that must be modified with the range of rows that contain the measure values on which the central line is based.

- *Moving Ranges*: The differences from one interval of time to the next.
- *Average Moving Range*: The average of the moving ranges. The shaded cell contains a formula that must be modified with the range of rows that contain the moving ranges on which the average moving range is based.
- *Upper Range Limit*: The upper range that appears in the mR chart.
- *Lower Natural Process Limit*: The lower natural process limit that appears in the X chart.
- *Upper Natural Process Limit*: The upper natural process limit that appears in the X chart.
- *Target Lower Natural Process Limit*: The lower natural process limit based on a target, if one is entered.
- *Target Central Line*: The central line based on a target, if one is entered.
- *Target Upper Natural Process Limit*: The upper natural process limit based on a target, if one is entered.

The following example illustrates the entry of a target:

Date	Measure	Central Line	Moving Ranges	Average Moving Range	Upper Range Limit	Limits Lower Natural Process Limit	Upper Natural Process Limit	Lower Natural Process Limit Target	Target Central Line Target	Upper Natural Process Limit Target
01/01/09	810.00	3,182.50				-24,900.10	31,265.10			
02/01/09	12,175.00	3,182.50	11,365.00	10,557.37	34,522.59	-24,900.10	31,265.10			
03/01/09	692.00	3,182.50	11,483.00	10,557.37	34,522.59	-24,900.10	31,265.10			
04/01/09	-4,507.00	3,182.50	5,199.00	10,557.37	34,522.59	-24,900.10	31,265.10			
05/01/09	-9,062.00	3,182.50	4,555.00	10,557.37	34,522.59	-24,900.10	31,265.10			
06/01/09	-7,022.00	3,182.50	2,040.00	10,557.37	34,522.59	-24,900.10	31,265.10			
07/01/09	-9,570.00	3,182.50	2,548.00	10,557.37	34,522.59	-24,900.10	31,265.10			
08/01/09	-11,308.00	3,182.50	1,738.00	10,557.37	34,522.59	-24,900.10	31,265.10			
09/01/09	19,710.00	3,182.50	31,018.00	10,557.37	34,522.59	-24,900.10	31,265.10			
10/01/09	19,140.00	3,182.50	570.00	10,557.37	34,522.59	-24,900.10	31,265.10			
11/01/09	11,000.00	3,182.50	8,140.00	10,557.37	34,522.59	-24,900.10	31,265.10			
12/01/09	-11,759.00	3,182.50	22,759.00	10,557.37	34,522.59	-24,900.10	31,265.10			
01/01/10	-11,810.00	3,182.50	51.00	10,557.37	34,522.59	-24,900.10	31,265.10			
02/01/10	24,842.00	3,182.50	36,652.00	10,557.37	34,522.59	-24,900.10	31,265.10			
03/01/10	19,878.00	3,182.50	4,964.00	10,557.37	34,522.59	-24,900.10	31,265.10			
04/01/10	2,297.00	3,182.50	17,581.00	10,557.37	34,522.59	-24,900.10	31,265.10			
05/01/10	-11,292.00	3,182.50	13,589.00	10,557.37	34,522.59	-24,900.10	31,265.10			
06/01/10	3,809.00	3,182.50	15,101.00	10,557.37	34,522.59	-24,900.10	31,265.10			
07/01/10	10,581.00	3,182.50	6,772.00	10,557.37	34,522.59	-24,900.10	31,265.10			
08/01/10	15,046.00	3,182.50	4,465.00	10,557.37	34,522.59	-24,900.10	31,265.10			
09/01/10										
10/01/10										
11/01/10										
12/01/10										
01/01/11										
02/01/11										
03/01/11									-10,000.00	20,000.00	30,000.00

FIGURE B.2

In this example, actual values only continue until August of 2010, and a target has been set in the future for March 2011.

The following example illustrates an XmR chart that displays a change in the central line and natural process limits:

Date	Measure	Central Line	Moving Ranges	Average Moving Range	Upper Range Limit	Limits Lower Natural Process Limit	Upper Natural Process Limit	Lower Natural Process Limit Target	Target Central Line Target	Upper Natural Process Limit Target
01/01/09	810.00	4,108.00				-30,984.46	39,200.46			
02/01/09	12,175.00	4,108.00	11,365.00	13,192.65	43,139.98	-30,984.46	39,200.46			
03/01/09	692.00	4,108.00	11,483.00	13,192.65	43,139.98	-30,984.46	39,200.46			
04/01/09	-4,507.00	4,108.00	5,199.00	13,192.65	43,139.98	-30,984.46	39,200.46			
05/01/09	-9,062.00	4,108.00	4,555.00	13,192.65	43,139.98	-30,984.46	39,200.46			
06/01/09	-7,022.00	4,108.00	2,040.00	13,192.65	43,139.98	-30,984.46	39,200.46			
07/01/09	-9,570.00	4,108.00	2,548.00	13,192.65	43,139.98	-30,984.46	39,200.46			
08/01/09	-11,308.00	4,108.00	1,738.00	13,192.65	43,139.98	-30,984.46	39,200.46			
09/01/09	19,710.00	4,108.00	31,018.00	13,192.65	43,139.98	-30,984.46	39,200.46			
10/01/09	19,140.00	4,108.00	570.00	13,192.65	43,139.98	-30,984.46	39,200.46			
11/01/09	11,000.00	4,108.00	8,140.00	13,192.65	43,139.98	-30,984.46	39,200.46			
12/01/09	-11,759.00	4,108.00	22,759.00	13,192.65	43,139.98	-30,984.46	39,200.46			
01/01/10	-11,810.00	4,108.00	51.00	13,192.65	43,139.98	-30,984.46	39,200.46			
02/01/10	24,842.00	4,108.00	36,652.00	13,192.65	43,139.98	-30,984.46	39,200.46			
03/01/10	19,878.00	4,108.00	4,964.00	13,192.65	43,139.98	-30,984.46	39,200.46			
04/01/10	2,297.00	4,108.00	17,581.00	13,192.65	43,139.98	-30,984.46	39,200.46			
05/01/10	-11,292.00	4,108.00	13,589.00	13,192.65	43,139.98	-30,984.46	39,200.46			
06/01/10	3,809.00	7,670.20	15,101.00			-37,743.68	53,084.08			
07/01/10	10,581.00	7,670.20	6,772.00	17,072.89	55,828.35	-37,743.68	53,084.08			
08/01/10	15,046.00	7,670.20	4,465.00	17,072.89	55,828.35	-37,743.68	53,084.08			
09/01/10	54,084.00	7,670.20	39,038.00	17,072.89	55,828.35	-37,743.68	53,084.08			
10/01/10	-9,735.00	7,670.20	63,819.00	17,072.89	55,828.35	-37,743.68	53,084.08			
11/01/10	-5,537.00	7,670.20	4,198.00	17,072.89	55,828.35	-37,743.68	53,084.08			
12/01/10	-7,958.00	7,670.20	2,421.00	17,072.89	55,828.35	-37,743.68	53,084.08			
01/01/11	13,225.00	7,670.20	21,183.00	17,072.89	55,828.35	-37,743.68	53,084.08			
02/01/11	1,722.00	7,670.20	11,503.00	17,072.89	55,828.35	-37,743.68	53,084.08			
03/01/11	1,465.00	7,670.20	257.00	17,072.89	55,828.35	-37,743.68	53,084.08			

FIGURE B.3

In the example, formulas in the cells that contain values highlighted in red were modified to create a change in the central line and natural process limits beginning in June 2010. Notice that the Average Moving Range and Upper Range Limit cells were left blank for June 2010 to create a break in the mR chart between the old and the new central line and upper range limit.

INDEX

About the Author

STEPHEN FEW has been working for 30 years as a teacher, consultant, and innovator in the fields of business intelligence and information design. Today, as the founder and principal of the consultancy Perceptual Edge, he focuses exclusively on data visualization. He teaches, speaks, and consults internationally with organizations of all types. More than anyone else working in data visualization today, he is respected and sought the world over for his ability to make data visualization accessible in simple and practical ways to anyone who wants to effectively understand and communicate the important stories that reside in quantitative information.

When he isn't working, he can usually be found—in or around his home in Berkeley, California—lost in a good book, savoring a fine wine, hiking in the hills, or instigating an animated discussion about the meaning of life.

Other books by the Author

In addition to *Signal*, Stephen Few has also written three other popular books on data visualization:

Show Me the Numbers
Designing Tables and Graphs to Enlighten

Information Dashboard Design
Displaying Data for At-a-glance Monitoring

Now You See It
Simple Visualization Techniques for Quantitative Analysis